Reusing the Resource
Adventures in Ecological Wastewater Recycling

"Less than two-tenths of 1 percent of the planet's water is drinkable, and 90 percent of that goes to uses in buildings, including flushing toilets."

–Natural Resource Defense Council

All the rivers run into the sea; yet the sea is not full; unto the place from whence the rivers come, thither they return again.

–Ecclesiastes 1:7 (King James Version)

"As California continues to struggle with its many critical energy supply and infrastructure challenges, the state must identify and address the points of highest stress. At the top of this list is California's water-energy relationship: Water-related energy use consumes 19 percent of the state's electricity, 30 percent of its natural gas, and 88 billion gallons of diesel fuel every year—and this demand is growing."

–California Energy Commission

"...It appears that the sweltering inhabitants of Charleston and New Orleans, of Madras and Bombay and Calcutta, drink at my well....The pure Walden water is mingled with the sacred water of the Ganges. With favoring winds it is wafted past the site of the fabulous islands of Atlantis and the Hesperides, makes the periplus of Hanno, and, floating by Ternate and Tidore and the mouth of the Persian Gulf, melts in the tropic gales of the Indian seas, and is landed in ports of which Alexander only heard the names."

–Henry David Thoreau in *Walden*

REUSING THE RESOURCE
Adventures in Ecological Wastewater Recycling

Carol Steinfeld
David Del Porto

ecowaters books
www.ecowaters.org

Proceeds from sales of this book help fund the programs of Ecowaters Projects, which informs the public about ecological wastewater recycling systems through tours, plans, workshops, and books.

Published by:
Ecowaters Books
www.ecowaters.org

Steinfeld, Carol
Del Porto, David
Reusing the Resource: Adventures in Ecological Wastewater Recycling

ISBN 978-0-9666783-2-1
1. Home 2. Water. 3. Environment/Science 4. Garden

Cover photos from top left: "The Gift of Water" fountain and biosculpture by Jackie Brookner in Germany (photo source: Brookner); Living Machine at Emmen Zoo, Holland (photo source: Living Machines, Inc.); Alison Flynn with urine-diverting flush toilet, Orleans, Mass. (photo: Edward Steinfeld). Second row: Canal Restorer in China (photo source: Todd Ecological); a graywater-irrigated rose in Oakland (photo: Mikka Tokuda-Hall); and Elevated Wetlands in Ontario (photo source: Noel Harding). Third row: Tanks of reused water for farm irrigation in Monterey, Calif. (photo: Carol Steinfeld); Walnut Cove wetland (photo source: Bill Wolverton); and indoor graywater planter at Wellfleet Audubon Sanctuary, Wellfleet, Mass. (photo: Carol Steinfeld)

contents

1. Introduction

It's Only Wastewater If It's Wasted

2. Principles of Ecological Wastewater Recycling

Growing Clean Water

Rhizospherics

3. Know the Flows

Source Separation

Viewing Wastewater as Not One Flow But Many Offers

Acknowledgments

Thanks to Howard Odum, the late ecologist who wrote the book on systems ecology; Bill Wolverton, NASA scientist who revealed the ability of plants to clean air and water; and Alfred Bernhardt, biologist and professor who showed the evapotranspiration abilities of planted wastewater systems.

Parts of this book were written at Mesa Refuge in Point Reyes, Calif. and on the houseboats of Jan Pehrson and Kristyan Panzica as well as Tad Thompson, all in Sausalito, Calif. Thanks to Dan Harper and Elva Del Porto.

And thanks to all herein for the adventures.

–Carol Steinfeld and David Del Porto

Foreword

BOB ZIMMERMAN, EXECUTIVE DIRECTOR
CHARLES RIVER WATERSHED ASSOCIATION

The notion that we are running out of fresh water in the same way we are running out of oil is troubling.

That notion demonstrates a stunning ignorance of how land and water work, and that ignorance accepts as gospel the logic of mechanical centralized water systems that take water from one place, use it in a second, and throw it away in a third. We are not running out of water; we just treat water like trash: We use it, make it dirty, and throw it away. As a consequence, we are drawing down streams and rivers with our demand and contributing to nutrient loading and hypoxic zones in our rivers and bays with our wastewater discharge.

Add to that the fact that something like eight percent of all energy generated in the U.S. is used to pump water around and treat it before and after we use it, and the folly of our engineered water systems is complete.

Unfortunately, infrastructure investments tend to beget infrastructure investments, so the likelihood that we will get water right, sustain ourselves, and restore our rivers and streams is far from given. More likely, we will perpetuate the centralized big pipe infrastructure we created. The proof is in the new fixation on desalination plants to resolve our "running out of water" problem. Think about that for a minute: In the age of global climate change, we are bent on burning hydrocarbons to strip salt out of seawater and pump that water uphill.

Reusing the Resource provides crucial philosophical and technical insights to help us get water right. It doesn't just address the "running out of water" issue; it addresses the root causes of the problems we've created with mechanical end-of-the-pipe treatment The approaches in this book will sustain us, help restore surface water bodies, reduce energy demand, reduce combined sewer overflows, help curb flooding, help build in resilience to drought, and add to urban open spaces.

It all sounds too good to be true, but it's not. As *Reusing the Resource* details, we possess the know-how to approximate the way land and water worked before we built all this stuff. If we start now, and use that single notion as our guiding principle so every water and wastewater infrastructure investment we make over the next 20 years moves us away from big pipes and towards the way land and water once worked, we will restore and sustain ourselves and the Earth.

About This Book

"Toilets in paradise" has been one of the more interesting themes of our work, and so there we were in the Micronesian islands, the essence of paradise in the middle of the Pacific Ocean, with the requisite waterfalls, rainforests, thatched-roof houses, swaying coconut palms, and warm coves alive with a kaleidoscope of fish.

But there was trouble in paradise, and one of the more populated islands showed it most acutely. Its shores were tinged with brown in many places. The harbor was dark and stagnant. Dead fish floated here and there. Algae clogged several inlets. Plastic trash piled up in the jungle which once consumed all the organic detritus of the islanders.

Coral reef die-off due to excess nutrients and other contaminants was well documented by Greenpeace International, which pinpointed wastewater as one of the main culprits. David Del Porto was hired to help design wastewater management solutions that could be easily duplicated by the locals and would contain and transform wastewater.

Although self-sufficient for thousands of years, the island's population increasingly relied on what the tanker ship brought from places far away. That included fuel to power the island's power plant, and even animal feed for the island's many pigs. Abundant rain fell on the island, but much of the population used tap water brought up from a fresh water lens under the island but above the saltwater of the ocean. This freshwater lens increasingly was less replenished, as rain was diverted from the ground by more asphalt roads and parking lots, and washed nutrients, contaminants, and debris into the shorelines and lagoons. It also was susceptible to pollution by septic systems that leached right into it. In the capitol city, a secondary wastewater treatment plant was subject to power outages, backups, and overflows during seasonal monsoons.

On an island, there is no faraway place to which to discard trash and wastewater. The destiny of all material flows is clear to see. When they are cycled back into the ecosystem, the result is a life-sustaining environment that doesn't require any outside energy but sunshine. But this cycle had been interrupted on this island. The effects compromised the health and wealth of its inhabitants, who relied on fishing and tourism, and clean water to thrive. Only 30 years earlier, islanders collected rainwater, and found that most of their discarded detritus—coconut shells, fish bones, and mats and baskets made of banana leaves and reeds—disappeared into the warm earth in short order.

That island could well be a microcosm for planet earth. Ultimately, all of our wastes end up in someone's ecosystem, whether it's our neighbors' water supply or the coral reef.

Increasingly, the solution seems to be found in methods and practices that borrow from the model of the waste and resource cycles we see in stable ecosystems. In thriving ecosystems, there is no waste—the outputs of one organism or function are the inputs of another. Energy is kept local, functions and organisms are many and diverse, cycles are tight (sources and outputs are close), and the processes and players adaptive. This results are systems that are resilient (able to withstand extreme events), stable, and low energy—offering the best chance of sustainability and even thrive-ability. To reframe wastewater management in an ecological perspective, the "wastes" that we want to "dispose" are used as valuable resources just as they are in nature.

This is a book about a wide range of wastewater-management solutions based on the ways thriving ecosystems work. It is about exciting opportunities to turn waste-treatment challenges into opportunities to provide energy, building materials, amenities, food, and cleaner water and air. It's also about success
stories and a reframing of the so-called "water crisis" as instead a crisis of lack of good strategy. This book is not an exhaustive review of these solutions nor is it a technical textbook with detailed test results and instructions for designing systems, the variables for which are vast. For that, we direct readers to sources as much as we can.

This book does not dwell on current water and wastewater inequities and a multitude of statistics about consumption that exceeds supply, because that is chronicled quite well by institutions such as WorldWatch and the Pacific Institute.

It is a menu of possibilities.

Taking an ecosystem-based approach to water and wastewater requires us to be systems thinkers who assess whole systems for opportunities, instead of looking for stand-alone, off-the-shelf, one-size-fits-all technologies. Sometimes, easy interventions in the system solve problems and reveal resources. The ecological opportunity is about revealing abundance. It's about "wastes" transformed into fuel, food, fiber, and of course, clean water for drinking, cleansing, growing, and making things. At the same time, it can provide beautiful planted solutions that compellingly sell themselves and enhance the quality of life of their communities.

We hope this book will inform, inspire, and broaden realms of possibility by sharing examples of innovation and ideas for this coming age that call on our best thinking to avert potential crises of water and energy scarcity and uncover undertapped sources of plenty. –CJS

A two-story solar greenhouse heats David Del Porto's home in Newton, Massachusetts. Inside, a two-tiered cascading pond with resident water hyacinth and koi fish treats graywater from the kitchen sink. A fig tree grows above it, its roots irrigated with the treated graywater. The graywater feeds a drip-irrigation system throughout the greenhouse. Outside, a 7-foot-long patch of hostas and evergreens manages graywater from the home's washing machine year-round.

Wastewater Terms to Know

Aerobic: Refers to the respiration process of organisms that use free molecular oxygen from air to release nutrients. Aerobic organisms (aerobes) are 10 to 20 times more efficient than their cousins, anaerobic organisms. Anaerobes live in anoxic (without dissolved oxygen) environment and must first digest oxygen-containing chemical and compounds, using up energy in the process.

BOD (Biochemical Oxygen Demand): A measure of biodegradable carbon used to measure the effectiveness of treatment. The volume of BOD in water is a measure of the amount of oxygen removed from a body of water to biologically degrade the carbon therein. As organic matter decomposes, it requires or "demands" oxygen. The removed oxygen will no longer be available to higher order animals, such as fish, which will die without enough dissolved oxygen. Adding oxygen to wastewater at 68°F (20°C) over a specific incubation period, then measuring the remaining dissolved oxygen, will yield the BOD of the sample in milligrams per liter.

Effluent: Treated, or partially treated, wastewater. See also Influent.

Excreta: That which is excreted by humans. Feces and urine are its primary constituents but also vomit.

Fecal coliform bacteria: Bacteria found in the intestinal tracts of mammals. Their presence in water or sludge is an indicator of possible presence of illness-causing pathogens. This can be from treated or untreated sewage, direct deposit of excreta, stormwater runoff, and even from plants and paper-mill effluent. High levels indicate risk of waterborne gastroenteritis. Fecal coliform bacteria are members of the family Enterobacteriacae, which include Escherichia coli, Citrobacter, Enterobacter, and Klebsiella species. Most are not pathogenic, but they are associated with pathogens such as Vibrio cholera bacteria, virulent forms of E. coli, and a form of Hepatitis virus found in the digestive tract. These organisms are less precise as fecal contamination indicators because many can live and reproduce in soil and water without a human host.

Influent: Untreated wastewater; the wastewater that flows into a wastewater treatment plant.

Secondary treatment: Biological and mechanical processes that remove dissolved organic material from wastewater, but not most nutrients.

Substrate: The material or substance providing a surface on which organisms attach, grow, and act. It also creates voids to store water and oxygen.

TKN (Total Kjehldahl Nitrogen): The combination of organically bound nitrogen and ammonia in wastewater. This must be released from the organic matter by a process of digestion prior to analysis. In most wastewater plants, biological activity breaks down the organic matter, releasing or consuming the nitrogen as energy in the process. Total nitrogen is the combination of organic nitrogen, and inorganic nitrogen (NH_4, NO_3, NO_2).

TSS (Total Suspended Solids): A measure of the amount of solids in the wastewater.

1. Introduction

It's Only Wastewater If It's Wasted

From Disposal to Utilization: A New Design Model

Our current common approach to wastewater management—sewers, central wastewater treatment plants, and septic systems—solved an immediate public health problem starting in the 1800s, allowing us to live in relative cleanliness and with lowered risk of excreta-transmitted disease.

But using drinking water—treated and delivered at significant expense—to dilute and dispose of another potentially valuable resource, human excreta, is getting expensive. To this we add industrial and household chemicals and stormwater drainage, then we pay a high cost to transport these combined effluents to a facility that attempts to separate all those constituents, clean them up to a degree mandated by federal law, and discharge the remaining water back into the environment—usually rivers, oceans, and the ground. In most cases, the same nutrients, pharmaceuticals, and toxic chemicals that went into the wastewater mix are still present in what leaves the treatment plant. Growing realization of the effects of this is prompting regulators to mandate further treatment—and that's making this "combine-dilute-treat-and-dispose" approach even more expensive.

Every year we learn more about the longer term effects of partial treatment and disposal, and that's driving more and stricter regulations. The Clean Water Act only requires the reduction of suspended solids, biological oxygen demand (BOD)*, and fecal coliform bacteria. But now, responsible regulators worldwide are mandating

the removal of nutrients, toxic chemicals, parasites, viruses, radioactive wastes, pharmaceuticals, and other constituents.

At the same time, planners are asking: In a world where drinking water is increasingly expensive and scarce, can we use this valuable resource for flushing toilets, washing cars, and irrigating landscapes?

This question is driving a fresh look at water uses and the various levels of cleanliness required for those uses.

It is clear that the answer is not a matter of more cleanup at the end of the sewage pipe. A more strategic and integrated solution is called for, based on a broad approach:
- Prevent pollution
- Conserve water
- Use local and diverse water sources
- Keep constituents separate at their sources
- Recycle and use its organics, water, heat, and nutrients

The High Cost of Disposal

The more that is learned about the impacts of wastewater nutrients on receiving waters, the greater the regulation required to improve the quality of it prior to disposal to rivers, streams, or groundwater. That means communities are facing the prospect of ever-higher and even prohibitive treatment costs.

This is prompting a reframing of the wastewater challenge. Instead of creating "wastes," a better strategy is to put these outputs to use, just as they are in nature's model. In balanced ecosystems there is no waste: The outputs of one organism are the inputs of another.

Increasingly, ecologically engineered systems that use root-zone interactions to treat wastewater are proving to be adaptive and cost-effective ways of managing wastewater and removing or using its unwanted constituents.

A new discipline, ecological engineering, is developing and designing these systems—optimized, controlled, contained, and monitored versions of systems in nature—which prevent wastewater pollution by using potential pollutants as nutrients in constructed ecosystems.

For treatment, the advantage of constructed natural systems is that they offer far more complex physical, biological, and chemical processes than any of our present technologies. In natural systems, most of the "treatment" occurs in the plant root mass, or rhizosphere. The rhizosphere serves as a dynamic bioplex, transforming the nutrients and complex organic compounds in wastewater into simpler forms the plants and microscopic animals use for energy and growth. These systems are robust and adaptive, adjusting to the changing nutrient and strength levels of effluent and ambient environmental factors.

Most conventional central systems offer only secondary treatment: reduction of suspended solids and BOD with optional disinfection. Most on-site systems offer primary treatment: separating solids from liquids and some biological activity, mostly in the soil to which they discharge. Natural systems often perform that, as well as a third stage, or "tertiary" waste treatment: removing, sequestering, or dissimilating toxic materials and using up the nutrients, so what flows out the

Ecological Treatment versus Mechanical Treatment

Natural or ecological treatment systems are those that mimic the ways wastewater constituents (water, particles, undesirable bacteria, nutrients) are removed in nature: through sequences of terrestrial and aquatic ecosystems such as soil, rootzones, marshes, streams, and ponds. Many of these biological processes also take place in conventional treatment systems, such as bacterial degradation of organic matter and nutrients.

As a treatment process, ecological systems are more robust than mechanical systems, because their complex diversity assures more complete utilization and transformation of pollutants. These systems are living and self-organizing, so their treatment adapts to changing wastewater strengths and constituents. In systems that use living plants as part of the process, the plants produce proteins and sugars as exudates that feed the treatment bacteria during times when there are little or no nutrients from sewage. This is especially significant for schools and seasonal facilities. Conventional systems will lose their bacteria and require re-inoculation before school startup.

Some marketers of ecological systems claim they are superior to conventional systems that employ large volumes of energy, chemicals, and mechanical equipment. Conventional systems might use more mechanization to move wastewater, screen it, clarify it, and filter it. Any chemicals used might be alum or polymers to sink (flocculate) solids for removal, as well as acetates or alcohol to add carbon, alkalinity additives, and finally, chlorine and a dechlorination agent to disinfect. Nearly all this might be used in a so-called ecological system, such as a sequenced aquaculture system. Treating large wastewater volumes in compact small-footprint systems, such as in cities and where land costs are high, requires more energy and processing to take the place of time, space, and utilization.

other end is significantly cleaner. How clean is a function of retention time, what and how many living organisms are at work, temperature, and the constituents of the effluent.

Some systems use up the effluent entirely, so nothing at all leaves the system except plants or compost. These zero-discharge approaches are typically installed where sensitive environmental conditions and geological conditions prevent disposal solutions.

Ecological Economics

Planners and developers are also finding that ecological wastewater systems can provide welcome amenities to their communities, serving as wildlife refuges, park-like settings, and abundant landscapes. In more advanced utilization schemes, they also provide irrigation and toilet-flushing water, biogas, living walls, heat, and plants for burning, building, and food.

Increasingly, sewage outfall pipes will be replaced with gardens, greenhouses, and tree plantations that grow fuel, fiber, construction materials, wildlife habitat, and appealing landscapes.

Pig and dairy farm wastewater will fertilize and irrigate crops used for manufacturing flooring and construction materials instead of polluting a river. A neighborhood's urine might be collected for hayfield fertilization, while its blackwater feeds a methane digester that powers lights and vehicles with biogas, and the residuals are composted. The warmth of its wastewater will be recovered to heat some buildings, and its graywater will be treated with engineered gardens then used for irrigation, toilet flushing, or aquifer recharge. All this will be financed, installed, and maintained by community management districts—at a substantial savings over the costs of operating a large central combined wastewater treatment plant, burning the sludge, and cleaning up polluted waters.

When the management challenge switches from disposal to utilization, the incentives for maintenance and improved public reception are built in.

Some are easy add-ons to current treatment systems and some involve a rethinking of how communities and developments are designed and engineered. The result is better economics, greater public health protection, wastes reduced, energy reclaimed, carbon sequestered, pollutants avoided, and cycles completed. That's a prescription for sustainability.

What a huge contribution Sir Joseph Bazalgette made to health when he built London's "seaward" system of pipes and tunnels, which today we know as "sewers." The problem now is that we've become too successful at making waste disappear. We have the illusion of clean homes because the by-products of city life are wisked out of sight and out of mind. But the population of the planet is much higher today, and certainly our cities are bigger than ever, forcing us to be aware of where our wastewater goes. Everything goes somewhere on this island planet earth, and that somewhere is someone's backyard and ecosystem.

–Stephen Salter

Conventional Treatment

"Most of my job is removing solids from water." –Wastewater treatment plant operator, Geneva, Ill.

Typically, conventional treatment refers to systems that have been used for decades to treat wastewater to meet treatment standards prescribed by local regulations. These systems are often categorized by the degree to which they remove pollutants the incoming wastewater, or influent.

Primary treatment: Primary treatment removes solids by screening, settling, or filtering out the large solid particles. After the trash and grit are removed, the wastewater still contains organic and inorganic matter in various forms and sizes. It is pumped or drained to a sedimentation tank where the volume is slowed to allow the solids to settle out. Advanced primary treatment means that more solids are removed, often by adding coagulants that coat the particles so they sink or float and are removed. This is called primary sludge or primary biosolids. These sludges or biosolids are then dewatered and disposed to landfills, incinerators, and composters; digested to produce methane (CH_4); or used as fertilizer.

Secondary treatment: Secondary treatment usually uses a biological process to remove up to 85 percent of the organic matter in sewage via bacteria naturally occurring in sewage to transform the organic matter into heat, carbon dioxide, and water vapor. This involves adding oxygen to the process to support the rapid growth of aerobic organisms and provide more surface area upon which certain bacteria can attach themselves (attached growth) and large vessels with aeration that provide the ideal conditions for aerobes that are suspended in the water column (suspended growth). Typical features of secondary systems include clarifiers, trickling filters, and activated sludge processes that return the fast-acting bacteria found in the sludge to the front of the system to inoculate the raw influent with beneficial microorganisms with forced aeration.

A coastal wastewater treatment plant manages several million gallons daily.

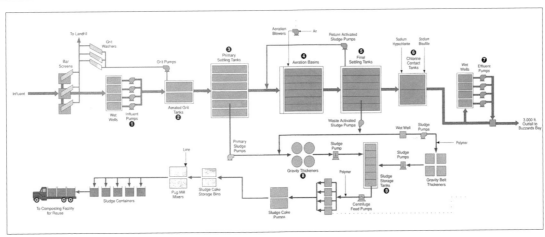

A secondary wastewater treatment plant with ocean outfall

Prior to discharge to the environment, the wastewater is disinfected by either chlorine, ozone, or ultraviolet light to destroy pathogens. In some jurisdictions, if chlorine is used for disinfection, it must be removed, or dechlorinated, to protect the receiving waters.

Tertiary treatment is an advanced stage that removes nutrients such as nitrogen (denitrification) and phosphorous, sometimes heavy metals, and perhaps in the near future, pharmaceuticals. Tertiary methods might involve the use of physical-chemical separation, sequencing batch and membrane bioreactors with reverse osmosis, or activated carbon.

Onsite wastewater treatment: Onsite systems (systems that are not connected to a sewer collection and central treatment system) typically comprise a conventional septic tank and leachfield. The septic tank usually holds a few days' worth of wastewater long enough so solids settle to the bottom (sludge) or float to the top (scum). Some of the solids ultimately liquefy. Septic tanks have one or two compartments with baffles to better keep the solids in the tank. There is little or no oxygen in the septic tank, so the microbiology inside is anaerobic. The somewhat clarified liquid then drains or is pumped to a distribution or "D" box that splits the flow and distributes it, usually by gravity, to a leachfield. This consists of rows of perforated pipes surrounded by gravel arranged as trenches or beds buried in soil suitable for percolating the liquid into the subsoil beneath the pipes. The septic tank provides primary treatment. Most of the treatment occurs in the leachfield and soil, where microbes further process the wastewater.

When regulations require additional treatment due to high groundwater or nearby streams, lakes, or other shoreline, or if the soil does not percolate well, advanced treatment systems are called for. These are like miniature secondary central treatment plants with additional technologies that add more surface area for biological activity as well as forced aeration to promote the more efficient aerobic microorganisms. Recirculating sand filters, packaged treatment systems with or without disinfection, are now common in North American communities where higher treatment is required.

What would an ecosystem do?

The following are four general guidelines to create ecosystems that are robust and adaptive, use energy for its highest purpose, sustain all their participants, and withstand catastrophes:

1. Increase cycling and reduce leaking of material and energy outside the cycles. Keep cycles tight and local.
Examples: Conserve water. Reduce transport of water and wastewater. Keep water as locally derived as possible (rainwater, recycled flows, etc.). Reclaim nutrients, water, organics, and heat. Reduce leaks. Start at the source.

2. Increase energy capture and flow: The outputs of one organism are the inputs of another.
Examples: Recycle nutrients in urine and blackwater to farms, animal fodder, fiber crops, and biofuel plants. Reclaim heat. Reclaim water. Reclaim heat in wastewater, while its organics produce biofuels and its nitrogen and phosphorus grow plants.

3. Optimize efficiencies.
Conserve water. Match water quality to its use. Keep flows separate for easier treatment. Disperse flows.

4. Diversify functions and resources and integrate them.
Examples: Use diverse water sources and a variety of modalities to treat effluent. Do not be afraid of the complexity of keeping flows separate: Manage them centrally. Use a variety of modalities for smaller flows rather than one large central system. Strive for multifunctionality. Use discharged water for cooling. Use ecological systems that double as air-cleaning landscapes.

Thanks to scientist Eric B. Schneider, author of *Into the Cool,* for contributing to these principles.

2. Principles of Ecological Wastewater Recycling

Growing Clean Water
Landscapes Replace Leachfields and Ocean Outfalls

Imagine a future in which gardens, greenhouses, and groves of trees replace sewage-discharge pipes and septic system leachfields. Wastewater will grow ecological tree plantations that provide food, fuel, fiber, construction materials, wildlife habitat, and beautiful landscapes. A piggery's nutrient-rich wastewater will fertilize a contained fiber tree farm instead of polluting a river. A house's wastewater will irrigate and fertilize its surrounding lawn, shrubs, and garden. Planted green roofs and green walls will collect and filter graywater and rainwater for use in homes.

That future is here. Increasingly, landscapes will do double duty as part of wastewater treatment systems that "grow clean water." The main drivers: Stricter wastewater regulations as well as rising water rates that could make drinking water too costly to use for irrigation.

Demand for ecological wastewater treatment will grow steadily as scientists and engineers find that landscape-based root-zone systems clean wastewater better than the conventional wastewater disposal leachfields, even in colder regions. Studies show 99.9 percent pathogen destruction in these systems.

At the Root of It All

Some use the term natural systems to describe plant-and-gravel-based wastewater systems, but this is a bit of a misnomer, as conventional treatment also uses natural processes. The ecological engineering field calls them "constructed ecosystems," because they replicate the kind of ecosystems that could process the wastewater components.

Some constructed ecosystems are always full of water, or saturated, and some are not. It all depends on the treatment goals, the soils, and the climate.

Treating wastewater involves destroying pathogens, reducing biological oxygen demand, filtering out particles, reducing or using up nitrogen and phosphorus, and stabilizing or disposing of toxins. All of this happens faster in constructed ecosystems than in conventional treatment systems. In a septic tank, for example, wastewater often is not treated; it is just settled. All pathogens, toxins, and nitrogen (mostly from urine) still drain from the tank into a leachfield gravel bed two to six feet underground and then into the soil, where some treatment occurs.

Constructed ecosystems keep effluent in the top 18 inches, which is the aerobic zone. Generally, a key advantage of the aerobic zone is more oxygen is present there. Oxygen-using or aerobic bacteria transform and stabilize wastewater 10 to 20 times faster than anaerobic bacteria that do not use atmospheric oxygen.

Another advantage of the biological zone is it can support plants. They establish the root system, or rhizoplane, where the real transformation occurs. The root system provides a home for beneficial bacteria to transform wastewater, dissimilating its constituents (what's in it) into forms that are taken up or consumed by bacteria, plants, and higher order organisms or released to the atmosphere. In the terminology of the wastewater treatment field, the substrate (coarse media such as gravel) and the roots behave like "fixed-film reactors," supporting microbes that attach to roots and substrate while preying on pathogens, turning nutrients into a form that plants can use, and converting nitrogen to a gas form that goes back to the atmosphere.

Plants also add air to the wastewater system through capillarity: Think of plant roots and stems as drinking straws. It is a commensal relationship. The pollutants feed the microbial community, and the microbes' byproducts are absorbed by the plants. In turn, the plants support the microbial community: Through photosynthesis, their roots receive nutrients—called exudates—in the form of complex carbohydrates (mostly sugars) that help maintain the microbes. As the roots decay, they provide the carbon required by the denitrifying bacteria to convert nitrates into nitrogen gas. (In conventional mechanical treatment systems, sugar is added for this purpose.)

Because they are living systems that are more biologically complex than most conventional systems, constructed ecosystems are also self-organizing and adaptive, providing responsive treatment that adapts to varying wastewater strengths and climate changes. Although constructed systems work faster in warm climates, they are successful in colder ones too. By and large, microbes do the work, and microbes are *poikilothermic*, which means their metabolic processes are directly proportional to the temperature. For every 19°F, their metabolic rate doubles. At 40°F, most microbes are dormant. But wastewater is usually warm, and microbial action generates heat, so treatment might slow during cold seasons but it rarely, if ever, stops.

Components of Wastewater Systems

Generally, a wastewater system starts with a collection system and settling tank, such as a sep-

tic tank. If the site requires more pretreatment before discharge, packaged-treatment plants, biofilters, or media filters can be used. These are essentially tanks containing aerators, peat, geotextiles (engineered fabrics), or complex plastic shapes that host microbes so more complex bacterial transformation of the wastewater can occur.

In a very ecologically oriented building, the wastewater flows can be kept separate: Water used for washing, called *graywater*, can be drained away separately so it can be used with less treatment than is required for high-nitrogen, higher pathogen toilet water, or *blackwater*.

The discharge then flows to a constructed ecosystem. This is often a bed or series of trenches full of substrate, such as gravel, peastone, sand, crushed concrete, and glass, or mulch. They can be various depths and lengths, lined or unlined, with or without outflow, and wet, damp, or mostly dry. They are planted with plant varieties chosen for their tolerance to the particular conditions and for their ability to take up water or add oxygen to the process. Further denitrification and disinfection might be necessary for sites that are environmentally sensitive whether due to high groundwater, rocky or clay soils, or proximity to shorelines.

Five Types of Constructed Ecosystems

Perhaps the best-known constructed ecosystem, although its name is often incorrectly used to describe the others, is the *constructed wetland*.

Typically chosen when there is plentiful land, constructed wetlands are planted beds or trenches filled with substrate and aquatic plants. They provide both aerobic and anaerobic conditions. To reduce phosphorus, wetlands require periodic plant harvesting; this should be performed before the onset of summer.

There are two types of constructed wetlands: *surface-flow* constructed wetlands and *subsurface-flow* constructed wetlands.

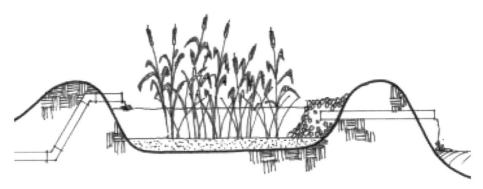

Surface-flow wetland (Illustration: Craig Farnsworth)

• In surface-flow constructed wetlands (also called free-flowing or surface water wetlands), water flows on top of the wetland. One can sometimes paddle boats on them but cannot walk on them. surface-flow wetlands are chosen where habitat that attracts wildlife, such as birds and fish, is desired. (However, remember that animals can contribute their own E-coli bacteria to the water.) Surface-flow wetlands also provide opportunities for waterfalls and water-flow features, enhancing both evaporation and aeration. Ideally, the wetland is designed so water flows fast enough that mosquito larvae cannot take hold in the moving flow; if not, mosquito-eating fish and birds should be present.

• With subsurface-flow constructed wetlands, water flows 3 to 8 inches under the wetland surface. The wetland can be walked on, driven over, even paved over, and integrated into pathways. Subsurface-flow wetlands work better than surface-flow wetlands in cold climates, because they are insulated from surface air and retain more heat. The sizing is about the same as freewater-surface flow wetlands. The deeper they are, the more anaerobic they are, which assists with denitrification (the conversion of nitrogen nutrients to nitrogen gas). Five-foot-deep and deeper subsurface-flow constructed wetlands are used for denitrification. A shallow wetland is more aerobic, promoting nitrification, which changes ammonia (NH_3) to nitrate (NO_3), a form of nitrogen accessible to plants, as well as evaporation. However, the shallower the wetland, the more susceptible it is to cold weather. Depending on the climate, designers might make a hybrid system with both shallow and deep parts.

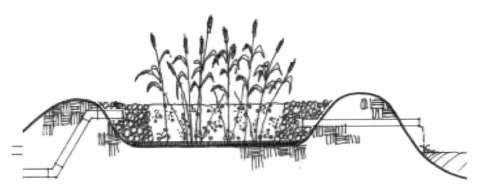

Subsurface-flow wetland (Illustration: Craig Farnsworth)

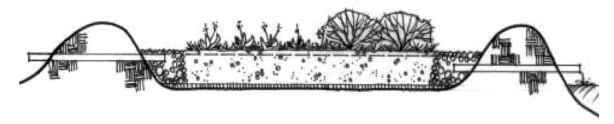

Planted rock filter (Illustration: Craig Farnsworth)

To reduce BOD, aerobic processes work best. The first 12 inches is the zone of aeration, so a wetland might start at 12 inches deep to reduce BOD and to nitrify and then head to greater depths of 19 inches to five feet for denitrification.

Planted rock filters are the least understood constructed ecosystems. Unlike their cousins, the constructed wetlands, these are more like constructed damplands and are not always saturated. Common in some southern states such as Arkansas, planted rock filters were designed and tested by NASA. Very flexible, they can be used for both stormwater and wastewater, and will work in both wet and dry conditions.

In fact, stormwater provides an ebb and flow that both flushes the system and optimizes all of the biological processes by providing a complex and diverse ecology. Because planted rock filters do not require wetland plants, they are more versatile for landscape features. Wastewater enters the system three to eight inches below the surface. Rain flows through the rock filter but does not collect and saturate, so nonaquatic plants, including shrubbery and vines, can be used.

Planted evapotranspiration systems, sometimes known as "recirculating wastewater ET gardens," are designed to use up wastewater. Evapotranspiration systems are typically trenches filled with gravel and distribution pipe and planted with especially thirsty plants, or phreatophytes. Evapotranspiration is a combination of evaporation and plant transpiration. Treatment is primarily unsaturated and aerobic. These systems are usually chosen to reduce or eliminate the cost of pumping a septic or holding tank on

Planted evapotranspiration system
(Illustration: Craig Farnsworth)

sites where effluent cannot be discharged.

Effluent first enters a tank and then is pumped into a bed of substrate such as gravel. Any effluent not evapotranspired is drained back to the tank. Because these systems are almost always specified where wastewater must be completely used up and not discharged, they are often lined. A good lining is a 20- to 40-mil. chlorine-free, low-density polyethylene film.

Sequenced aquaculture systems, with brand names such as Solar Aquatics Systems, Living Machines®, and EcoMachines, are sequences of aquatic tanks (think of aquariums filled with plants) and indoor constructed wetlands that are often enclosed in greenhouses. They replicate vertical pond systems. Inside the tanks, aerators bubble in oxygen and agitate the mix. At their best, they resemble silos of flowers, foliage, and even trees. They are chosen when advanced treatment is required, such as for water reuse in a building. These systems can also process sewage solids or sludge.

Methods of distributing the outflow from these systems (if there is any) include:

• Subsurface irrigation: After treatment, effluent is distributed under six inches of suitable pervious soil, typically by pressure-dosed, small-diameter perforated pipe or through flexible drip tubing with emitters. Remember that drip irrigation is for dispersal, not treatment, and effluent must be extremely well filtered to prevent clogging of emitters.

• Surface irrigation: Effluent is disinfected and distributed to the soil surface, typically

When Plants Pollute
How wastewater-derived nutrients can cause aquatic pollution

When the nutrients in wastewater—usually from human excreta—are discharged or leach into ponds, lakes, streams, and seas, the effect is like pouring fertilizer into the water. The nutrient balance is upset, resulting in a proliferation of organic matter, namely aquatic plants such as phytoplanktons and algae. These plants, both as they live and when they ultimately die, use oxygen in the water. This can upset the oxygen balance and deprive other aquatic life of necessary oxygen. These plants also reduce the clarity of the water, preventing sunlight from reaching the depths. Populations of shellfish, coral, fish, and many other aquatic organisms can be limited by eutrophication. The state of low oxygen is called "hypoxia," and is a well-known problem along the seacoast of the Gulf states, where fertilizer runoff from farm fields is considered the primary culprit. Along the east coast of the U.S., wastewater that is discharged to sea, leached from septic systems to the ground, or run off via stormwater from surfaces are big sources of nutrient pollution of water. From Chesapeake Bay in Maryland to the Baltic and Black seas, nitrogen pollution is considered a major environmental and economic threat. Due to different bacterial processes, nitrogen is the nutrient that causes most trouble in saltwater. In freshwater, phosphorus is the more troublesome nutrient or "limiting nutrient." However both are nutrients of concern and should be put to work to grow food, fuel, and fiber, not ecological liabilities.

A pond choked with algae is evidence of fertilizer—nitrogen and phosphorus—in the wrong place.

through conventional sprinklers or other clean-water irrigation systems.

To complete a full, ecologically elegant, onsite watervmanagement strategy, add plumbing for reuse. Treated and disinfected effluent from constructed ecosystems can be filtered, possibly disinfected, and piped back to the building for use in toilet flushing and water for evaporative cooling systems.

Success Factors

Designers must take into account the "design flows" from the building, a volume that is set by legal authorities as the target treatment volume. Precipitation (rain, snow) and temperature must be factored in as well as leaf drop. Fallen leaves add carbon to the system, unless leaves are raked off. Many wetlands fail because the substrate is too small, causing clogging. Designers are currently using 3/4- to 3-inch gravel. The larger the pore spaces (the spaces between the gravel), the lower the chances of clogging.

Plant Palettes

Plant palettes for constructed ecosystems ideally include *facultative* plants (plants that do not mind having their roots wet or dry). In wetlands, only *obligative plants* (the roots of which must be always wet) are used. Start with fast-growing plants such as grasses and water hyacinth for a base of workhorse plantings, then accent with showy plants. Look for broad-leafed plants; the more leaf area there is, the more evapotranspiration takes place. Vines allow for maximum leaf area with minimal footprint.

Select plants that look good and smell good so that people will take care of them, as well as plants that do not need care, such as bamboo and holly. For shallow constructed ecosystems installed to remove nitrogen, running bamboos such as *Phyllostacys aurea, Phyllostacys bisetia,* and *Phyllostacys nuda* work well. Line the system with

40-mil. polyethylene lining, which has been proven to prevent spreading of bamboo.

If wetlands are planted with reeds, the foliage might need to be harvested to remove carbon. Where treated wastewater is discharged to surface water, such as lakes and ponds, both the leaves and the roots should be harvested periodically to remove the phosphorus. For cold-climate systems, select evergreens that are cold tolerant. Hardy evergreens do not go dormant in the winter, so their root zones are active even in the snow.

As in any landscape, 10 to 40 percent of the plants might have to be replaced during the start-up period. Also, there is a start-up time before optimal treatment is seen: The warmer it is, the sooner treatment revs up. Beware that constructed ecosystems often self-select what

GOOD BOOKS

Treatment Wetlands, Robert Kadlec and Robert Knight; CRC Press, 1995

Small and Decentralized Wastewater Management Systems, Ronald Crites and George Tchobanoglous; McGraw-Hill, 1998

Growing Clean Water: Nature's Solution to Water Pollution, Bill Wolverton; Wolverton Environmental Services, 2001

Wetland Design: Principles and Practices for Landscape Architects and Land Use Planners, Robert L. France; W.W. Norton, 2002

Constructed Wetlands in the Sustainable Landscape, Craig Campbell and Michael Ogden; Wiley & Sons, 1999

Start at the Source, Tom Richmond; Bay Area Stormwater Management Association, 1999

Water Use and Conservation, Amy Vickers; WaterPlow Press, 2002

Sewage Solutions, Nick Grant, Mark Moodie and Chris Weedon; Centre for Alternative Technology, Wales, UK, 2005

plants work best. Your plantings might be replaced by local plant varieties. Sometimes these offer even better treatment because they are better adapted to the local conditions.

In constructed ecosystems with no outflow that are sheltered from precipitation, and so are not regularly flushed out, salt can build up. This can be flushed out with water, or the system can be planted with halophytes. These are plants that take up salt, such as mangrove and tamarax (salt cedar).

Who Can Design Them

In most states, a local permit is required for an onsite wastewater system treating less than 10,000 gallons per day (gpd). (Many states, such as Massachusetts, establish a mandatory design flow per bedroom of 110 gpd.) Wastewater systems managing more than 10,000 gpd require a groundwater discharge permit unless the discharge is to surface waters, which are regulated by federal requirements. Many states certify professional engineers to design smaller systems; however, exceptions can be made for those who can demonstrate the necessary skills. Some states, such as Iowa and Vermont, allow anyone to design wastewater systems, as long as they comply with state guidelines.

As states regulate for higher treatment of wastewater, constructed ecosystems will become increasingly common treatment modalities. Civil engineers will seek out the services of landscape designers to help them integrate these solutions into their clients' sites. The distinction between landscape and wastewater treatment system will soften, as the ability of soils, substrate, and plants to clean wastewater and stormwater runoff is recognized.

As this landscape-based approach replaces the current plumbing approach to wastewater management, constructed ecosystems will be commonly called on to clean effluents as well as provide valuable plant products and beautiful landscapes.

Ecological Engineering

When looking for ways to achieve water sustainability and better ways to treat wastewater, we can first look to an organizing principle of life on this planet, the ecosystem. Ecosystems work optimally when energy and material flows are kept cycling through, so that the outputs of one part of the system are the inputs of another. This means energy and resources stay in the system, producing no waste, and they don't have far to travel. A defining feature of ecological systems is that they self-organize according to the specifics of their resource bases, and they adapt as these change. For wastewater

Wastewater treatment plant operator Scott Sargent compares the incoming wastewater (left) in a sequenced aquaculture system to the treated effluent (right). (Photo: Living Machines)

treatment, an ecological system can handle the varying strength of flows.

We can engineer systems based on these ecosystem principles. The term "ecological engineering" was first coined by Howard Odum, a professor of systems ecology in 1962. Ecological engineering, he wrote, is "Those cases where the energy supplied by man is small relative to the natural sources but sufficient to produce large effects in the resulting patterns and processes."

Managing water in human communities to sustain the highest quality of life for the lowest cost works best by using an engineering model based on the ecological paradigm. Ecological engineering of all aspects of an urban or industrial site can transform it into an efficient (and therefore profitable) watershed. When possible, we must recycle, reuse, or utilize effluents and source local water. Using them strategically, such as for landscape irrigation, flushing toilets, and evaporative cooling, helps save both water supply and wastewater treatment costs—and prevents effluents from becoming pollution.

Just as "reduce, reuse, and recycle" has become the credo of responsible solid waste management, this strategy will become more obvious and important to the world's population than presently can be imagined. As treatment modalities, ecologically engineered wastewater systems are self-organized, modeled on how the components of wastewater are managed in nature (with soil, plants, and organisms), use wastewater as a sustaining consumable (water, nutrients, organics), and are as close as possible to wastewater sources and ultimate users of their outputs (biomass, food, biogas, organics).

Rhizospherics
How Plants and Soil Substrates Clean Wastewater

Many assume that plants somehow "filter" or "purify" wastewater by consuming it. It's not that simple. A complex biological community of inter-actions occurs between plants, roots, the substrates (soil, gravel, sand, peastone, crushed concrete, even recycled and tumbled glass) they grow in, and the micro- and macroorganisms that inhabit this bioplex to remove organics, pathogens, and even salts, heavy metals, and toxins. This bioplex is called the rhizosphere.

The rhizosphere is that area that surrounds and includes the roots, the soil, and most significantly the microcosm of bacteria, algae, fungi, actino-mycetes, worms, and other organisms that live there. This area appears to be simply substrate and plant roots, but there is more than meets the eye. Viewed under a microscope, the area is teeming with life in what ecologists call "commensalisms" that include bacteria and nematodes feeding on plant cell detritus. Plants exude sugars and pro-teins through their roots to nourish the bacteria and other organisms. Protozoa and other organ-isms feed on the bacteria. Fungi and actinomycetes produce antibiotics such as penicillin and strepto-mycin that contribute to the health of the plant by suppressing disease.

Wastewater enters the rhizosphere, and its sedi-ments, chemicals, nutrients, and possibly pathogens attach to the substrate and roots in a process called adsorption.

Both the substrate and the roots are habitat for a wide and diverse population of microorgan-isms that use these wastewater components as energy sources.

Bacteria ingest and break apart the components with enzymes and transform them into different forms that the bacteria can use for food or miner-als to construct their cells. All living organisms (animals or plants) take in food and excrete what is not necessary for their survival. Organisms excrete components that other organisms use, such as nutrients that plants absorb into their roots and up the xylem and phloem (the transport system in the plant stalks) to make energy for the plant cells that make leaves, fruits, and seeds.

What the plant does not need, it excretes through the stoma underneath its leaves as oxygen (O_2), water vapor, and even some methane (CH_4).

Some plants act as a catalyst and dissimilate complex molecules and compounds to forms bacteria can use as energy and to transport min-erals and other chemicals into the bacteria. Higher order organisms (protozoa, rotifers, para-mecium, and others) eat the bacteria and syn-thesize amino acids that are the building blocks of the proteins used by plants and animals to build their cell walls.

Biofilm
The complex biological community of microor-ganisms living in a watery environment substrate and plant roots is often referred to as a biofilm. This biofilm is so thin that free metabolic oxygen

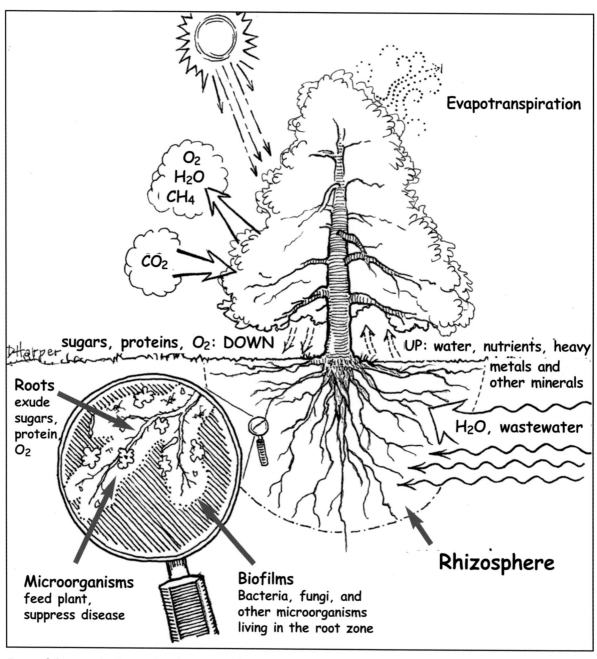

Evapotranspiration

O_2
H_2O
CH_4

CO_2

sugars, proteins, O_2: DOWN

DHarper

UP: water, nutrients, heavy metals and other minerals

H_2O, wastewater

Roots
exude sugars, protein, O_2

Microorganisms
feed plant, suppress disease

Biofilms
Bacteria, fungi, and other microorganisms living in the root zone

Rhizosphere

Some of the complex interactions between a plant and the rhizosphere (Illustration: Dan Harper)

from the atmosphere can dissolve in the water to support aerobic organisms.

The plants send down complex sugars and proteins (exudates) to the roots. These both act as lubricants (so roots can better penetrate soil) and feed the organisms that transform nutrients and other chemicals to forms that can be used by the plants. Plants also send oxygen to their roots, some of which is for the roots and some for the bacteria living in the roots.

You might say the bacteria and fungi feed the plant, and the plant feeds the bacteria. It's a commensal relationship.

The wastewater volume, temperature, and strength and the amount of plants and total surface area of the substrate determine how long the wastewater has to be in the rhizosphere to transform the wastewater constituents to forms that are beneficial or at least environmentally benign. The more organisms in the biofilm, the more complete the transformation.

Pathogens

Ecological wastewater systems offer diverse and robust ecologies that host many more opportunities for pathogens and other wastewater constituents to be reduced than in most conventional treatment systems.

In ecological wastewater systems, most pathogens are dissimilated and transformed into food via enzymes of microorganisms living in the biofilm. That food is consumed by higher order organisms and plants. Some of this food and other bacterial secretions are "sorbed" or adsorbed onto substrates and roots until other organisms dissimilate them with their enzymes.

Some pathogens attach to sediments and some move around in the wastewater.

Can pathogens taken up by plants endanger the health of anyone who eats them? Plant roots, because they are semipermeable to minerals, nutrients, and water and usually will reject anything else, do not appear to transport any human

pathogens that survive the rhizosphere.

Then there are environmental factors for pathogen destruction: Pathogens usually do not live long outside the host. When they find themselves in an environment that's not suited to them, they die off quicker than they would have by old age, which would ultimately happen.

Viruses are ultramicroscopic particles of nucleic acid (DNA and RNA) coated with protein. They invade cells and replicate themselves by tricking the cells to multiply.

Many viruses can cause illness but some do not. All viral diseases are caused by viruses but all viruses are not disease causing.

Bacteria are microscopic prokaryote life forms that are organisms without a cell nucleus or any other membrane-bound organelles. Most are unicellular, but some prokaryotes are multicellular. They are one of the most plentiful and smallest units of life that we know about.

Some bacteria, such as Escherichia coli (E. coli), cause disease, and some are beneficial to their hosts, helping to synthesize vitamin K, among other good things.

Fecal coliform (FC) bacteria presence is commonly measured to determine the degree to which any pathogens from humans are in wastewater. A common requirement for treatment is an FC count of less than 200 parts per liter.

Toxics Treatment in the Leaves

Some toxins in wastewater, such as chlorinated hydrocarbons, can be removed by photodegradation through the leaves. The plant takes up these components into its leaves where the sun's ultraviolet rays pass through the leaves and photodegrades the toxins.

Salts

Most plants reject salts, because they can result in hypertension that hinders the plant's circulation of water and nutrients. But some ion-accumulating plants accumulate salt ions and transport them to the surfaces of their leaves and recombine them in specialized glands as solid salts. With some of these salt-uptake plants, called excretive halophytes, you can actually see the salt crystals on their surfaces. Saltwater cordgrass, also known as saltmarsh hay, is one such example. Another is Salt cedar (Tamarix spp). In this plant, dropping salt is a survival mechanism: When it drops its leaves, it makes the surrounding soil too salty for competing plants. To avoid that, you should harvest these plants, such as by allowing animals to graze them. (You might call this a green salt lick.)

A salt mine in Poland harvests its salt from vines that take it from the earth.

Temperature

Temperature is another factor that determines how long the wastewater should be retained in the rhizosphere and how large the wastewater system should be for best treatment.

The warmer the system, the faster the biological activity. Consider the Q10 coefficient: for every 10°C (19°F) temperature increase above 4.4°C (40°F), the biological processing rate doubles. For the roots, the limit is about 48.9°C (120°F), but certain thermophiles (heat-loving organisms) thrive above 45°C (113°F), and some live at or even above the boiling point of water! For practical purposes, biological zero, or the temperature at which most living organisms are no longer capable of metabolizing nutrients, is 4.5°C (40°F); 30°C (86°F) is about the optimal temperature for biochemical rates of reaction for beneficial microbes in wastewater, especially nitrifying bacteria.

If the wastewater is cold, it will have to be treated in a larger system with a longer retention time. Conversely, if it is warmer, the retention time can be shorter and the system size smaller.

Aerobic versus Anaerobic

Certain plants add some oxygen to the rhizosphere. However, the preferred way to add oxygen to the process is to diffuse air into the waste-

water, thereby dissolving oxygen into it. This can be accomplished by aerating the liquid or aerating the substrate's many air spaces. These spaces are referred to as pore spaces or void spaces. They are also a measure of wastewater retention capacity.

How aerobic the rootzone is depends on the design: A saturated (filled with water) system that is deep and without aeration will be primarily anoxic (lacking dissolved oxygen). One that is large and shallow, so the surface-to-volume ratio is high to expose more of the system to oxygen, will be primarily oxic (containing dissolved oxygen). Microorganisms that live in a primarily oxic habitat are said to be aerobes. Those that thrive in an anoxic environment are said to be anaerobes. Some organisms can switch from anaerobes to aerobes depending on their environment; these switch-hitters are called facultative organisms.

The smaller the substrate is, the smaller the void spaces, so there is less space for oxygen and more likelihood of clogging. Scientist Bill Wolverton in his book *Growing Clean Water* observed that many failures of constructed wetlands were due to clogging from lack of prefiltering of the wastewater and too-small substrate. He recommends 3/4- to 3-inch size substrate. In addition to gravel, substrates such as expanded shale, recycled plastic or glass, and crushed construction waste products are specified for their abilities to host biofilms.

Aerobic bacteria process wastewater faster than anaerobic bacteria, sometimes 10 to 20 times faster, because aerobes use free oxygen efficiently. Anaerobic bacteria must get their oxygen by eating other organisms or matter with oxygen in it. This requires more energy, making anaerobes less efficient.

For this reason, many system designers use different means of oxygenating their systems. Some use aerators on the bottom of the system to bubble air into the roots in the style of fluidized beds. Some circulate the wastewater to a tank then back into the treatment bed or from one treatment bed to another and back. Some drain down one system completely to pull the wastewater through the substrate and roots. This process allows full contact with the biofilms and prevents the biofilms from becoming "flabby," according to Living Machines engineer David Maciolek. Many systems now feature two treatment beds that are used alternately, so the sludges and detritus in one bed can be transformed and consumed by aerobic microorganisms without disruption by new inputs while another bed is in use. This also allows easier harvesting of the biomass in the inactive treatment bed, helping to remove carbon and nutrients (notably phosphorus) and restore some breathing room in the system.

Macronutrients (NPK)

The main macronutrients in wastewater targeted for treatment are the same nutrients we buy as garden fertilizer and measured as NPK: Nitrogen (N), phosphorus (P), and to a far lesser degree, potassium (K). That's because these nutrients, when discharged to groundwater or surface water, are pollutants—a resource in the wrong place.

Nitrogen is both a pollutant and wonderful fertilizer necessary for plant cell growth. It can cause unwanted plant growth in water. It also causes trouble when it enters the public drinking water supply such as in groundwater. Nitrates in the water can cause diseases such as methemoglobinemia, which in humans interferes with hemoglobin's ability to transport oxygen to the cells. Those with compromised immune systems and the very young and elderly can be affected by it. When infants are affected, it is called blue baby syndrome.

There are two ways to deal with nitrogen, and both are biological in nature: Turn it into gas or use it to feed plants.

Most nitrogen in domestic wastewater (as opposed to industrial or agricultural wastewater) is in the urine flow alone—as much as 90 percent. Nitrogen is from the animal and plant protein that we eat and can't use and so excrete as excess. It is also from the reabsorption of dead cells in our bodies.

Nitrogen

In human urine, several compounds contain nitrogen, including uric acid and creatine, but the main source is a large molecule called urea [CON_2H_4 or $(NH_2)_2CO$]. This organic compound contains ammonia, carbon, nitrogen, oxygen, and hydrogen.

As urine drains from toilets and urinals through pipes, certain bacteria that live on the inside of the pipes (helicobacter) transform the larger molecules into ammonia and ammonium (NH_3 and NH_4) with an enzyme called urase. In the wastewater system, the NH_3 and NH_4 first meet aerobic bacteria (nitrosamonas) that metabolize them and excrete nitrite (NO_2) as a byproduct. Living close to these bacteria are aerobic bacteria (nitrobacter) that use this byproduct as an energy source. Nitrobacter bacteria use oxygen and excrete nitrate (NO_3); that's plant fertilizer. This process is primarily nitrification and is carried out mostly by aerobic bacteria and a few facultative bacteria. The process requires some carbon, which the plants and the wastewater itself provide.

We pay a fortune to buy nitrogen fertilizer to grow green lawns, corn crops, and so forth, yet we spend another fortune to dispose of it in wastewater. In fact, many plant-choked ponds and coastlines are eutrophied (oxygen-deprived) from the over-use of lawn and agriculture fertilizers.

Most wastewater system designers want to turn nitrogen into gas. Denitrification requires an anoxic (both aerobic and anaerobic) environment that hosts anaerobic bacteria that eat nitrate (which contains some oxygen) and excrete nitrogen gas into the atmosphere. Certain bacteria that are denitrifiers use the carbon from the nitrate (NO_3) and release it as gas, N, and some nitreous oxides. This bubbles up through the anoxic environment and returns to the atmosphere, which is already 78 percent nitrogen. (Some warn against adding more nitrogen to the atmosphere, which is already heavily laden with nitreous oxides from sources such as coal-burning power plants.)

Constructed wetlands can provide the aerobic-anaerobic conditions that denitrify. Very generally, the upper layers are aerobic. Deeper down, the oxygen diminishes and anoxic conditions prevail; this is where anaerobic bacteria thrive. All the work is done by denitrifying and nitrifying bacteria (heterotrophic bacteria, paracoccus denitificans, and thiobacillus denificans) living in the substrate. This is a "redux reaction," which is shorthand for oxidation-reduction reaction. The plants can help by adding oxygen as well as bio-available carbon in the form of exudates.

If the pH is too high, the nitrogen is released as ammonia gas (NH_3). The nitrifiers (converting ammonia to nitrate) require high alkalinity relative to the amount of BOD, but bacteria like pH-neutral environments. Often, baking soda (sodium bicarbonate) is added to increase the alkalinity.

Plants can take up some of the nitrogen; it all depends on what is planted. Nutrient-hungry grasses such as bamboo could consume significant nitrogen before it can be released as gas. Other plants do not use a lot and are chosen mostly for the appropriateness of their root system as habitat and their ability to add oxygen to the process.

Phosphorus

Phosphorus (P), which can be a problematic nutrient when discharged into freshwater, is a macronutrient for plants. Typically phosphorus is removed from wastewater via "precipitation" by adding a coagulant that attaches to the phosphorus and sinks it to the bottom from which it is removed.

Phosphorus is also bio-accumulated in plants.

In wetlands, phosphorus from wastewater is "adsorbed" (attaches to) on roots and substrate. But if it is not removed, the wetland reaches a saturation point at which it will no longer "sorb" the phosphorus. This can take a few years, but the net effect is that eventually the substrate and roots must be removed and replaced, an expensive undertaking for large wetlands.

If you plant crop grasses that will be harvested, you can remove a lot of phosphorus. Many wetland managers say this is not economically feasible unless there is a market for the harvested crop, such as saltmarsh hay. Plant wetlands and other constructed ecosystems with plants with a harvest value, so the economic incentive to remove the phosphorus is built into the system.

Potassium

Potassium (K) is another macronutrient that behaves similarly to phosphorus and is also bioaccumulated by plants. Potassium is a key plant macronutrient, but it is not a pollutant of great environmental concern at this time.

Evapotranspiration

Another process at work in constructed ecosystems, mostly above the rhizosphere, is evapotranspiration (ET). A combination of evaporation and a mechanism called transpiration, evapotranspiration occurs inside a plant leaf as it gets rid of excess water by metabolizing it as vapor. About 1200 BTUs of energy are required by a plant to evapotranspire one pint of water.

Typically, 10 percent of water is lost through surfaces, including plants, depending on wind, moisture in the atmosphere, temperature, and surface area. This varies considerably from cold climates to hot and dry climates.

Some systems are designed to completely evapotranspire all the water away. However, in water-scarce areas, the goal is to reclaim the water and so the system must be designed for water retention.

Start-Up

A few wastewater researchers have stated that plants do little to enhance wastewater treatment in gravel beds. Usually their test periods are no more than one or two years. For a robust rhizosphere to to achieve significant performance, a period of at least three years is needed.

Living plants add resilience and the ability to adapt to new inputs or environmental conditions in wastewater systems: The rhizosphere changes according to the strength and components of the incoming flow. They add complexity and diversity of treatment, offering the best opportunity for destroying pathogens, removing nutrients, and dissimilating sediments and chemicals.

At the same time, planting with valued plants—whether for aesthetics, fiber, construction material, food, biofuels, biomass for energy, or more—both embeds an incentive to maintain these systems and offsets their costs, while providing oxygen, sequestering carbon and nutrients, cleaning the air, and buffering temperatures.

Hormones and Pharmaceuticals

The next frontier of wastewater treatment is dissimilating hormones and pharmaceuticals, so they do not enter the ecosystem and affect both humans and wildlife.

Female hormones, mostly from estrogen hormone-replacement therapy for menopausal women, are showing up in waters worldwide, possibly resulting in secondary sex characteristics in fish and other animals. Hormones, as well as endocrine disruptors (chemicals that hinder or stimulate hormonal reactions), can also be carcinogens.

One study suggests that constructed wetlands reduce hormones in wastewater. Analyzing hog farm effluent both before and after passing through constructed wetlands, researchers found the wetlands reduced estrogenic activity by 83 to 93 percent, which is below the concentration known to cause effects of concern. Estrogen, estradiol, and testosterone concentrations were measured.

Nutrient removal was measured to ensure the wetlands were functioning in a manner commonly reported in the literature. Nutrient removal levels were typical for treatment wetlands: TKN 59 to 75 percent and phosphate 0 to 18 percent.

The wetland consisted of marsh areas with cattails and a pond area that was both open and covered with floating vegetation.

Pharmaceuticals comprise a wide range of chemicals. Researchers addressing this treatment challenge must first examine the components of the most commonly used drugs, including antidepressants and heart medication. Conceivably, the same complex interactions in constructed ecosystems could also dissimilate and render benign the ingredients of pharmaceuticals.

Reference
Estrogenic Activity and Steroid Hormones in Swine Wastewater through a Lagoon Constructed-Wetland System. Nancy W. Shappell, Lloyd O. Billey, Dean Forbes, Terry A. Matheny, Matthew E. Poach, Gudigopuram B. Reddy, and Patrick G. Hunt. *Environmental Science Technology;* 2007

Phytoremediation
Using Plants to Detoxify Land and Water

Phytoremediation is another example of plants cleaning the environment: Sunflowers remediate radiation, rendering it less harmful. Mustard plants remove lead from soil. Ferns pull arsenic from the ground.

Phytoremediation increasingly is used to clean sites contaminated with heavy metals and toxic organic chemical wastes, such as solvents, petrochemicals, wood preservatives, explosives, and pesticides, as well as organic contaminants. It is most useful when contaminants are within the top 3 to 8 feet (1 to 3 meters) of soil.

Phytoremediation combines the Greek word *phyton* (plant), with the Latin word *remediare* (to remedy) to describe how certain plants, working with soil organisms, transform contaminants into forms that are harmless and even valuable.

Phytoremediation can work in three ways: (1) uptake, accumulation, and removal by harvesting the plant; (2) dissimilation with biodegradation, and (3) photodegradation. It takes advantage of plants' nutrient-use processes: taking in water and nutrients through roots, transpiring water through leaves, and supporting microbial life around their roots that metabolizes organic compounds, such as oil and pesticides.

Plants also can absorb, accumulate, and sequester toxic trace elements such as heavy metals (lead, cadmium, and selenium, for example). In some cases, plants contain 1,000 times more metal than the soil in which they grow. Heavy metals are closely related to the elements plants use for growth. In many cases, the plants cannot tell the difference between the two, according to plant scientist Dr. Ilya Raskin. Metals can be harvested with the plant. For example, mustard greens were used to remove 45 percent of lead in a Boston playground. The plant-sequestered lead was removed and safely disposed of. Raskin also demonstrated the ability of certain mustard plant varieties to remove metals such as chromium, lead, cadmium, and zinc from contaminated soil. Mustard plants and pumpkin vines were used to remove metals from a New Jersey pen factory site. Using plants to accumulate lead results in much less material for disposal than removing the contaminated soil, the usual method. Composting the removed plant material can add another stage in the breakdown of contaminants.

Raskin used hydroponic plant cultures (plants suspended in open water) to remove toxic metals from liquid waste streams. Hydroponically grown sunflowers were used to absorb radioactive metals near the Chernobyl nuclear site in the Ukraine as well as at a uranium plant in Ohio.

When large thirsty plants such as willows, poplars, and bamboo are used, the aim is to move as much water as possible through them so that they take up higher volumes of the contaminants. In 1991, the Miami Conservancy District Aquifer Update, No. 1.1 reported that a single willow tree can transpire more than 5,000 gallons (19 cubic meters) of water on a hot summer day. One hectare of a plant such as Spartina (saltwater cord grass) evapotranspires up to 21,000 gallons (80 cubic meters) of water per day. Once the heavy metals are absorbed, they are sequestered in the plants' leaves or roots where they are either metabolized or can be harvested.

At a former lumberyard site in Florida, scientists found ferns drinking up arsenic in the soil and storing it in their fronds. Arsenic, which is poisonous to humans, is used to pressure-treat lumber and to make semiconductor chips. It was used to manufacture insecticides and chemical weapons. The fronds of Pteris vittata, or brake fern, can be clipped or the entire plant can be dug up and disposed.

Bioremediation Booster: *Bioremediation* uses soil microorganisms to dissimilate organic contaminants, and has been used both as an onsite process and offsite for soil removed from contaminated sites. Plants can accelerate bioremediation by stimulating soil microorganisms, because plants' rootzones (the rhizosphere) have many more metabolically active microorganisms than unplanted soil. Plants sustain large microbial populations in the rhizosphere by transporting oxygen to their roots and secreting substances such as carbohydrates and amino acids through root cells and by sloughing root epidermal cells, both of which help feed the microorganisms. Root cells secrete mucigel, a gelatinous substance that lubricates roots to help them penetrate the soil during growth and also supports the microbial life dwelling in the roots.

Salt: Salt-tolerant plants, called halophytes, have reduced salt levels in soils by 65 percent in just two years in one project involving land damaged by brine runoff from oil and gas production in Oklahoma. After the salt was reduced, the halophytes died, and native grasses, which failed to thrive when the soil was too salty, naturally returned and replaced the salt-converting plants.

Rice cultivation has been shown to improve saline soils. According to Iwasaki, the salt content of an 8- to 18-inch (5 to 10 cm) of soil was reduced to less than one-fifth the original salt content after a single year of rice cultivation. Rice plants improve soil by accumulating salts in their shoots (George, 1967).

Phytoremediating Buffers: Plants can be used to prevent the spread of contaminants off site by wind and water. Strategic plantings, sometimes called planted buffers, are used to catch contaminants and keep them out of surface and groundwaters.

Greenhouse Gasses: Soil microorganisms help decompose organic residues and release plant nutrient components such as carbon, nitrogen, potassium, phosphate, and sulfur. A significant amount of the carbon dioxide (CO_2) in the atmosphere is used by plants to synthesize organic matter, primarily through photosynthesis. This transformation of carbon dioxide, and the subsequent sequestering of the carbon as root biomass, helps reduce global climate change by balancing the effect of burning fossil fuels that result in the greenhouse gasses that create it.

The conventional method of soil cleanup is to remove the soil and contain it in a hazardous-waste landfill or incinerate it. Phytoremediation can destroy organic contaminants rather than simply immobilizing or storing them. When the contaminant does not dissimilate, such as metals, the plants can be harvested and put into a smelter to recover valuable metals such as silver. Or they can be contained where they cannot harm health, such as the very underground mines from which the metals originally were extracted.

Mining contaminants with plants that dissimilate them into benign compounds that can rejoin a healthy ecosystem certainly qualifies as an ecological best management practice.

References

Kumar, P. B. N. A., V. Dushenkov, B. D. Ensley and I. Raskin. "The use of crop brassicas in phytoextraction: a subset of phytoremediation to remove toxic metals from soils." Proceedings of Ninth International Rapeseed Congress: Rapeseed Today and Tomorrow. D. Murphy (ed.) the Dorset Press, Dorchester, UK. 1995

Blaylock, M.J., S. Dushenkov, D. Page, G. Montes, D. Vasudev, and Y. Kapulnik. Phytoremediation of a Pb-contaminated brownfield site in New Jersey. In Emerging Technologies in Hazardous Waste Management VIII, Extended Abstracts for the Special Symposium, Birmingham, Alabama, Industrial & Engineering Chemistry Division, American Chemical Society, September 9-11, 1996.

Salt, D. E., R. C. Prince, I. J. Pickering and I. Raskin. "Mechanisms of cadmium mobility and accumulation in Indian mustard. Plant Physiology."109, 1427-1433.

Economic Research Service, USDA Industrial Uses. September 1996

R. Henchman, M. Negri and E. Gatliff "Phytoremediation using green plants to clean up contaminated soil, groundwater, and wastewater," Argonne National Laboratory, 1998

K. Ruder, www.genomenewsnetwork.org August 6, 2004

Iwasaki, K. "The effectiveness of salt-accumulating plants in reclaiming salinized soils." Japan. *Journal of Tropical Agriculture* 31:255. 1987

George, L. Y. "Accumulation of sodium and calcium by seedling of some cereal crops under saline conditions." *Agronomy Journal*. 59: 297. 1967

SOURCE SEPARATION AND RECYCLING

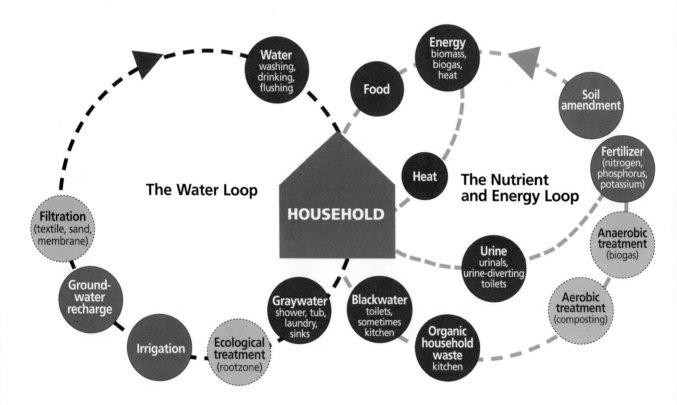

Adapted from a graphic by Otterwasser

3. Know the Flows

Source Separation

Viewing Wastewater as Not One Flow but Many Offers
A New Frontier of Treatment and Reuse Opportunities

Consider the wastewater flows that might be discharged every day from a two-bedroom house inhabited by a family of two adults and two children:

- Perhaps 40 gallons of slightly soapy water from bathroom sinks

- Maybe 15 to 37 gallons of water, toilet paper, and excreta from two bathrooms

- About 36 gallons of graywater from four daily showers

- Four gallons of greasy washing water and four gallons of rinse water from the kitchen sink and dishwasher

- More than 50 gallons of graywater from a load of laundry in the washing machine (Vickers, *Water Use and Conservation*, 2002)

Each flow has unique characteristics, including biological oxygen demand (BOD), total suspended solids (TSS), nitrogen (N), phosphorus (P), surfactants (from soaps), and a fecal coliform count. Some of these constituents are easier to treat than others. Some are more diluted and some are more concentrated—even from the same appliance.

The toilet water, or blackwater, by far represents the greatest source of fecal coliform and other pathogens and certainly the highest concentrations of nitrogen and phosphorus.

Other flows, such as sink and washing machine graywater, are relatively benign, with high BOD content and lower fecal coliform counts to treat.

Yet all these flows ultimately combine and leave the house in one pipe to a septic system or municipal sewer, where considerable energy, time, and money are spent to separate these constituents for treatment–then disposal or recycling.

The advantage of the decentralized onsite treatment is that flows are kept small, local, and separate from effluents that require more technical treatment, such as industrial discharges laden with heavy metals or toxic chemicals.

Yet perhaps we don't take the decentralized, onsite recycling approach far enough: Instead of thinking of end-of-pipe flows, we might replumb a building and keep separate the various flows for effluent-specific treatment.

Effluent-specific treatment takes the onsite advantage to its ultimate efficiency: treating each dilute or high-strength flow with a modality best suited to its specific constituents and treatment goals. Besides offering treatment advantages and possibly cleaner discharges to soils and groundwater, this approach also provides more and easier opportunities to reuse water and nutrients.

The most popular example is treating graywater, a relatively easy-to-treat effluent, to irrigate gardens and landscapes.

The tradeoff is more pipes, possibly more hardware, and more complexity. However, this complexity offers advantages for effectiveness. In the broader sense, it is nature's way, just as a robust and resilient ecosystem consists of a diversity of systems working interdependently and locally at a scale appropriate to the site environment, with resource and energy cycles kept tight. In the same way, a home's water and nutrient flows—a micro-watershed—can be more strategically managed to be used onsite to the benefit of the humans, flora, and fauna on that site.

In the future, a home's landscape will likely feature two or more wastewater treatment components disguised as gardens or groves of trees.

The result: cleaner effluents, fewer potential pollutants, more reuse opportunities, and possibly lower costs overall.

To illustrate the advantages of source separation, consider the menu of specific flows and effluents from a building and some specific treatment methods:

Blackwater
Urine and "yellow water"
Graywater

Blackwater (Toilet Water)

The highest-strength flow, with the highest nitrogen and phosphorus (mostly from urine content), organics, total suspended solids, and potential pathogens in the form of human excretions is blackwater, all that is flushed from toilets. More than any other domestic wastewater, this flow is the most complex and mostly what comes to mind when one thinks of brown-gray, malodorous wastewater.

Diverting blackwater isolates most of the pathogens. Blackwater can be thick and concentrated, but at about 80 percent water, it is liquid enough to effectively drain to a sewer or septic system without a boost from other flows.

Interestingly, blackwater, with or without urine, has a better carbon-to-nitrogen ratio and

pH for aerobic and anaerobic treatment when kept separate from graywater.

Faster biological processing occurs with aerobic microorganisms. Without the addition of graywater, blackwater is far more aerobic. In the future the septic tank might be replaced with aerobic biofilters that dewater blackwater and expose it to air, either passively or mechanically. The result is a more finished and dry product that is lighter to transport via truck to composting facilities.

Today's composting toilet system technology essentially operates in this way. An in-ground version might look like a tank containing an air diffuser, much like some of the aerobic treatment systems on the market. In many states, installing a composting toilet system allows for a smaller leachfield, often a significant cost savings that also minimizes disruption of the site and its trees.

The organics and pathogens are more quickly degraded and the product is more suited to land application thanks to the absence of heavy metals.

Further possibilities include using microflush toilets and dual-flush toilets to further reduce toilet-flushing water. The Aquatron Separator from Sweden even uses a centrifugal component to separate solids from the flushing water.

Blackwater treatment options include:
• Septic systems
• Reduced-size advanced aerobic systems with air diffusers, specialized media, and the like.
• Composting toilet systems
• Smaller holding tanks

Urine and Yellow-Water

Urine accounts for as much as 90 percent of the nitrogen and 50 percent of the phosphorus in a household's wastewater, yet it represents only about one percent of the total flow. Because nitrogen pollution of coastal waters is a growing problem for many communities, isolating this source is advantageous.

Nitrogen leaves the human body in the form

of urea, creatine, and other components—mostly as a result of consumed protein unused by the body. Yet urine is nearly always pathogen free in a healthy population. The most likely exceptions are hepatitis C, leptospirosis, and schistosomiasis. However, Swedish research shows that these are deactivated with a short period of containment and usually are not measurable hours after excretion.

Urine leaves the human body separately, and that provides opportunities to collect it. The easiest, already common in public facilities, is with waterless and water-flush urinals. Another plumbing fixture, the urine-diverting toilet, is a newcomer to the wastewater field. Mostly manufactured in Europe and Mexico, these feature a separate drained compartment cast in the forward interior of the toilet bowl to which urine naturally expresses when the user sits (or aims carefully while standing). Urine-diverting toilets are available as both waterless and flush models.

Separated from water, urine in dry weight has an average 11-1.5-2 NPK (nitrogen-phosphorus-potassium) value in western populations, although this varies widely depending on diet.

Some Swedish urine-diverting models flush with .03 gallons for urine (almost half a cup) and .8 to 1.3 gallons for solids. The Europeans coined the term yellow-water for the urine-flush water mix.

Yellow-water offers a blend of water and nitrogen ideal for plants, so it is a natural for fertilizing and irrigating landscapes.

Swedish and Mexican schemes collect urine and diluted urine to fertilize animal fodder crops, such as alfalfa and barley. Studies show that when urine is contained in tanks for six months, any pathogen that were present (usually due to fecal contamination in the toilet) die off.

Urine's nitrogen is in the form of ammonium (NH_4) when it leaves pipes and must be converted to nitrate, a form plants can use, by nitrification. This is best done with an aerobic system or by applying it to aerobic well-mulched soil with a high carbon content. This provides the carbon-to-nitrogen ratio and aerobic processing that fixes the nitrogen, so it doesn't convert to gas and waft away. For the wastewater system designer, a more regulatory acceptable approach is to create a constructed ecosystem that either grows away the nitrogen or denitrifies it.

To denitrify, or convert the nitrogen to gas, urine can be treated with a conventional denitrification tank system or via a small constructed wetland, both of which provide the combination aerobic-anaerobic, or anoxic, conditions to denitrify it.

Urine is a low-phosphorus fertilizer compared to purchased mineral fertilizers, making it ideal for phosphorus-sensitive sites near streams, ponds, and lakes where phosphorus is considered the nutrient that can cause the most problems. (In saltwater, it is nitrogen.) Generally, nitrogen is the primary nutrient for growing green leaves.

Designers of wastewater systems for day-use facilities, such as schools, might look at yellow-water collection or urine-growaway gardens, because these facilities often have nitrogen-rich flows without sufficient carbon (from feces and toilet paper) or graywater (from showers and washing machines) to provide the biochemistry necessary to treat it effectively.

Urine and yellow-water treatment possibilities:
- Smaller denitrification systems
- Intermittent and recirculating sand filters
- Constructed wetlands
- Planted evapotranspiration systems
- Collection and storage for on-site or off-site use such as for grass, hayfields, and tree farms, as well as composting operations that need a nitrogen boost

Graywater

Graywater is water used for washing that drains from sinks, showers, tubs, and washing machines. Blackwater is everything that leaves toilets. In many states, blackwater is kitchen sink drainage due to the presence of blood, solids, and greases.

Toilet and kitchen sink discharge account for about 40 percent of an average American home's wastewater. That means a little over half of household wastewater is graywater, with an average BOD (biological oxygen demand) of about 140 mg/gal (530 mg/l) and low volumes of particles (TSS or total suspended solids), nitrogen, and pathogens (see Table 1 in the Appendix) compared to blackwater.

More than Soapy Water

Graywater's relative clarity prompts many property owners to assume it is benign and essentially clean. So they drain it directly (and illegally) from their washing machines onto their backyard lawns and gardens. Plants appreciate this steady pulse of warm water, but over time, odors and fiber mats build up as the BOD and particles decompose too slowly.

Graywater contains stuff worth treating: Skin, hair, oils, salts, fibers, and other organics, such as BOD or bioavailable carbon from soaps, condi-

tioners, cooking oils, etc., that can clog the soil as well as irrigation emitters. BOD can cause odors when graywater is in open containers or applied to surface soil. Also, graywater can contain fecal coliform, especially if it was used to wash bodies, diapers, and the like. Although the health risk is usually low, it does warrant prudence and treatment. It is not simply soapy water.

To a lesser extent, salty soaps, high-strength cleansers, disinfectants, and chlorine bleach can pose challenges. Graywater can be slightly alkaline depending on the pH of tap water, cleaners, and other substances used.

All this points to a need for some treatment: Filter, float, and settle out particles and fibers, reduce BOD, and destroy pathogens. Clarification and disinfection is required only when it is applied to soil.

General categories of graywater-treatment systems are: shallow leachfields, drip irrigation, planted evapotranspiration systems, a branched-drain system, filtration, disinfection, and various versions of wetlands and ponds.

There are four general approaches to treating and using residential graywater.

Common features of most graywater-irrigation systems are filters to remove particles, subsurface irrigation components (graywater should not be exposed), and porous substrate or aerators to promote fast-acting aerobic biological

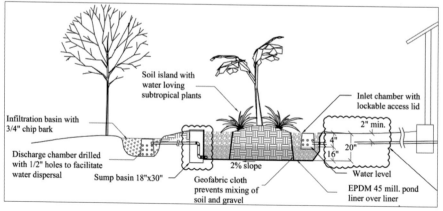

The appeal of making graywater visible compelled some Californians to design this and similar systems with small constructed wetlands that take the place of surge tanks while treating graywater before it flows to woodchip-filled trenches around trees. (Graphic: EcoHouse of Berkeley)

Soil island with water loving subtropical plants

Inlet chamber with lockable access lid

2" min.

Infiltration basin with 3/4" chip bark

4"
20"
16"

Discharge chamber drilled with 1/2" holes to facilitate water dispersal

Sump basin 18"x30"

2% slope

Water level

Geofabric cloth prevents mixing of soil and gravel

EPDM 45 mill. pond liner over liner

activity, and hearty plants. The plants work to use up nutrients, evapotranspires the water, and provide root systems to support the biota that will treat the graywater.

Start with...

Some state regulations require a full-size or smaller septic tank for the graywater system, even if a full-size tank is already in place for a conventional combined septic system. A septic tank can be replaced with the following for better performance and safety:

• **Filtration:** It is best to first prefilter and pretreat graywater so it does not clog soil, substrate, or drip-irrigation emitters. Many plans for simple systems, even those permitted in California, suggest using nylon stocking filters to filter out particles. This will be sufficient for 240-micron fibers, however, many cloth fibers are about 40 microns in size, including

PolarFleece and other nonbiodegradable fabrics.

The Filtrol 160 and other filters offer a more controlled filtration with 40-micron cloth filters encased in cartridges. These should be rinsed off outside. For best results, use a 120-micron filter followed by a 30-micron filter.

• **Grease interceptors** (grease traps) are key for kitchen sinks and dishwashers where greasy pans are washed. Greasy sludge is even found in bathroom sinks. Grease interceptors resemble miniature septic tanks with baffles to hold back floating grease, oils, and particles so they can be skimmed off. Their drawback is owners' unwillingness to maintain them by removing the top and skimming out the floating scum layer. Be sure to install one sized to the volume of hot greasy water typically discharged. One restaurant replaced an entire graywater bed because its grease trap was too small for the volume of hot, greasy water that drained from its dishwasher. Greasy graywater overflowed the

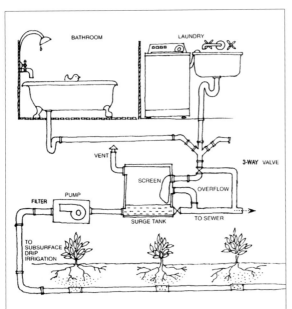 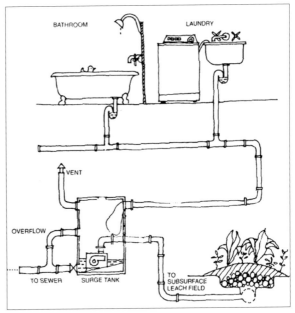

Two simple graywater systems preapproved by the state of California: One is drip irrigation (left) and the other is a shallow planted leachfield. (Illustrations: California Graywater Guide)

interceptor and coated the graywater planter bed's gravel and plant roots with grease.

• **Surge tank:** A surge tank—whether it is a septic tank or a 55-gallon drum—helps equalize flow to the system and avoid overflowing. It also helps cool the water, and it can serve as a grease trap if the scum layer is periodically skimmed. Pumps and filters are often installed in the surge tank.

• **Diverter valve:** Another key component for peace of mind is a three-way diverter valve. This allows diversion of graywater to a septic system or sewer, if the system is overloaded with graywater (or rainwater) or if the content of the graywater is a concern, such as when toxic cleansers are used.

• **Substrate and plants:** Chunky growing media (substrate) promotes fast-acting aerobic biological activity, and hearty plants. The plants work to use up nutrients, evapotranspire the water, supply root systems to support beneficial bacteria, and provide beauty. A system designed without substrate must rely on aerators, contact with the containing surfaces, or the receiving soil to treat the graywater.

A common mistake is using soil in a graywater-treatment system. Graywater contains a lot of bio-available carbon from soaps, detergents and body oils, which can clog soils, creating anaerobic conditions and odors.

Generally, graywater is a lot of water and a little bit of carbon and not much nitrogen, unless a lot of diapers are washed. Adding a little nitrogen improves the carbon-to-nitrogen ratio of the graywater so the microbes get a more complete diet and work faster. Fertilizer can be added or even a little bit of urine.

Most state regulations will not allow you to irrigate edibles, especially root crops such as

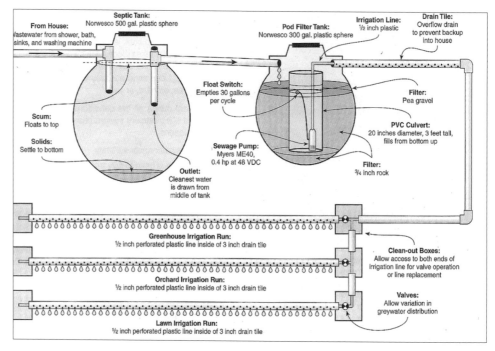

A SymBiosis graywater system in Minnesota features a septic tank followed by a gravel filter that doubles as a pump basin. Graywater is diverted via switch valves to one of three destinations depending on the season: a greenhouse, an orchard, or the lawn. (Graphic: Home Power Magazine, David Abazs)

carrots and potatoes, with graywater, unless it is disinfected. The logic is that root crops will come in contact with wastewater that might carry human pathogens.

Some Graywater Systems

Subsurface irrigation of non-edible plants is the easiest way to use graywater from cost, legal, and public health standpoints.

Distributing graywater below the soil surface provides some treatment of the graywater via soils or substrate while distributing graywater to plant roots. This prevents contact by humans, animals, and other vectors that can carry disease organisms. It also distributes water closer to plant roots and minimizes evaporation and temperature losses.

• **Small shallow leachfields**, such as one of California's two state-approved designs, are usually series of gravel-filled trenches in which perforated pipes distributes graywater. California requires a one-foot depth to allow root access and evaporation. Some get creative and provide various inlets in which they insert a hose to direct washing machine discharge to where it is needed most.

• **Planted evapotranspiration systems**, such as the Recirculating Washwater Garden, are typically used where all graywater must be used up, such as on an environmentally sensitive site where regulations forbid any wastewater discharge. Much like lined and sometimes insulated leachfield trenches or beds, these systems are sized to use up the graywater through evaporation and plant transpiration.

• **Subsurface wetlands and plant-rock filters** are sometimes saturated systems planted with plant species that like their roots wet. When used for graywater alone, these systems might fail due to a nitrogen deficit. One solution is to add urine, composting toilet leachate, or liquid nitrogen fertilizer.

• **Drip irrigation** to disperse graywater to an entire lawn is the ideal of many property owners who seek to use every drop to avoid using tap water at all. But this approach requires pretreatment or filtering as well as reducing the BOD to avoid clogging the emitters. To do that, you can filter the graywater through an irrigation filter or sand filter or aerate it (mechanically or with a constructed ecosystem) to reduce BOD. System designer Heather Shepherd in California installs moisture sensors that signal to a diverter to direct graywater to dry spots in a landscape.

GRAYWATER-USE ACCESSORIES

Filters
Filtrol 160
www.septicprotector.com

Clivus Multrum graywater filter
www.greywater.com

Drip irrigation equipment
Rewater
www.rewater.com

Netafim
www.netafim.com

Rainbird
www.rainbird.com

Diverter valves
Grainger
www.grainger.com

• **Mulch-basin node systems** pipe graywater to basins of mulch or woodchips, ideally next to trees and other plants that can use it. The advantage is that no filtration is required, as long as the basins are monitored and woodchips periodically replaced. System designer Art Ludwig calls his system "the branched drain system" for its branching distribution pipes that disperse graywater to basins of woodchips throughout a site.

• **Surface-flow wetlands and ponds** are usually chosen where storage of graywater for irrigation or a pond feature is desired.

GREYWATER, GRAYWATER OR GRAY WATER?

Cross-referencing articles and regulations pertaining to graywater is made more challenging by the various spellings of the term used by regulators and advocates. The term may have been imported from the United Kingdom and Australia; hence the spelling "greywater" with an "e" instead of an "a" still follows the term in the United States. In the mid-1990s, the Environmental Protection Agency (EPA) established the spelling "graywater" as a rule for its use in its documents. New Mexico uses the grammatically correct "gray water"; however, if read out of context, this can be construed to mean water that is gray. Just as the term "blackwater" is maintained as a compound of the two terms, so "graywater" establishes the term as a fixed meaning for this effluent. A consistency of spelling would go a long way to help with cross-referencing of information on this topic. Ideally, the EPA-sanctioned spelling, "graywater," will be adopted by all states and advocates.

• **Surface drip and spray irrigation** always require disinfection, such as with an ultraviolet unit or reverse osmosis, must be approved in all states except New Mexico, which allows surface application of graywater up to 250 gallons daily without disinfection. Pretreatment is critical to prevent clogging of emitters and the receiving soils. Disinfection allays pathogen concerns but does not treat organics (BOD), which can cause odors as they decompose slowly.

• **Recycling for toilet flushing and outdoor washing** is the ideal of many, especially as green-building rating systems, such as LEED (Leadership in Energy and Environmental Design), gain favor. This requires full water treatment with filtration and disinfection.

Toilets flushed with untreated graywater have clogged with accumulations of soaps and oils. Even graywater filtered with high-end reverse-osmosis systems often still has a yellowish color. Recycling graywater for this purpose will require special permitting in the United States.

• **Recycling for drinking/potable use** requires advanced treatment that is expensive and elaborate enough to discourage this use in all but the most idealistic or water-scarce places. Disinfection kills most potential pathogens of concern, but water will still be cloudy with particles and BOD.

State Regulations

Few states specifically address graywater systems beyond specifying a full- or reduced-size leachfield for its dispersal, often with a full-size septic tank.

Prompted by intermittent droughts, California was the first state to broadly allow two irrigation treatment options for graywater: a reduced-size shallow leachfield and a drip-irrigation system. A sizing formula is keyed to flow, although the state's climates and geology vary widely. These designs are state approved, but final approval rests with local health agents. Preliminary soils and depth-to-groundwater tests are required.

A common complaint with California's regulations is that they are too conservative. They essentially require constructing a duplicate leachfield to an existing septic leachfield, and the expense of that are not immediately recovered by avoided water costs.

New Mexico adopted a graduated standard that allows irrigation of graywater of up to 250 gallons per day without a permit, if general guidelines are followed including overflow to a septic system or sewer. (This volume is more than most households will produce.) After that, the graywater must be disinfected. Water used for washing anything soiled with excrement is categorized as blackwater.

Arid Arizona's Type 1 Reclaimed Water General Permit allows private residences to irrigate with untreated graywater of less than 400 gallons per day if it is discharged at least five feet above the groundwater table. The law calls for filtration but does not specify the means.

Water-rich Massachusetts developed guidelines for graywater use, mostly to promote better overall onsite treatment by reducing the volume of fecal-contaminated water. Graywater must be dispersed under nine inches of soil and pretreated via a septic tank or a graywater filter approved by the state's plumbing board.

What About Freezing?

Graywater enters a system warm, and biological activity in the system generates heat. However, shallow dispersal will not work year round in colder climates. Dispersal to lower depths is needed.

Graywater systems abound, many installed without permits. More will likely come on line as laws relax to allow less costly graywater systems. Studies show that graywater has little, if any, significant pathogen risk. As water gets too expensive to throw away, graywater systems will likely become "wastewater treatment as usual."

See the appendix for more information about using graywater from commercial facilities

A planted evapotranspiration system uses graywater from the washing machine. They can function even in cold climates if they are planted with hardy evergreens and perennials such as bamboos and holly. (Illustrations: Dan Harper)

Filtering Graywater

Graywater, before it is discharged to drip irrigation lines, soil, or substrate, such as gravel, should be filtered to remove particles and fibers that can clog pipes and emitters, jam valves or pumps, and prematurely fill up the void spaces in the soils of your planting beds. This is in addition to reducing BOD (including carbon and greases) that can also clog. Some designs, such as wetlands and direct discharge to trenches of woodchips that are periodically replaced, might not need this step. Some system owners skim fibers, particles, and greases out of their surge tanks.

Nylon stocking filters often are not sufficient. Nonbiodegradable and buoyancy-neutral particles, such as the plastic lint from polyester, nylon, and polypropylene fabrics, are increasingly accumulating and clogging leachfields, drip-irrigation systems, and soils. Today's microfiber and microfleece fibers, are made of recycled plastic bottles. Washing machines agitate fabrics and break the plastic fibers into pieces that are often 30 to 40 microns in diameter and length. One micron equals one thousandth (0.001) of a millimeter or 0.00004 inches. In the past, when fabrics were made of only biodegradable fabrics, such as cotton, wool or cellulose-based rayon, a simple nylon stocking was a cheap adequate filter.

Several filters are available. Filters are graded by pore size, which tells you the size of particles they let through.

• **Textile filters:** For filtering laundry washwater, 160 microns is minimum and 30 microns is preferred. It is best to use filters in series, so the finer filter does not get clogged every day. The Filtrol 160 connects to washing machines. It features either a 160- or optional 30-micron removable filter cartridge inside a transparent plastic case with a screw-off lid. According to the manu-

facturer, the 30-micron cartridge filter will remove more than 99 percent of solids (lint, hair, pet fur, sand, clay, etc.). It will also reduce oils and soap scum.

• **Insect screens and septic tank effluent filters:** These pore sizes are too large (3/16-inch) for filtering out the nonbiodegradable fibers. However, septic tank filters, such as those made by companies such as Zabel, catch hair, rings, coins, and so forth.

• **Granular activated carbon (GAC)** used for water filters can be very effective as polishing filters. They can be expensive to install and the carbon cartridges require frequent replacement.

• **Sand, anthracite and diatom swimming pool filters:** Whether they are up-flow, down-flow, recirculating or fluidized bed, or the tank types sold in catalogs, these filters can be effective, depending on sand grain size. However, they need to be backwashed periodically to clean them. Some larger systems do this automatically. Most will not filter out the nonbiodegradable 30-micron particles, because the sand grain size is too large.

• **Peat filters:** Compacted fine peat provides small pore spaces and has a unique ability to allow contaminants to adhere (adsorb) to the peat fibers.

• **Utrafiltration and reverse osmosis filtration:** Increasingly, reverse-osmosis filtration is gaining favor despite its high cost for equipment, energy, and maintenance. This is a pressure-driven separation process that pushes graywater across and through a semi-permeable membrane with pumps. They can remove bacteria, salts, and more. Most commercially available membranes are made from polymers, ceramics, metals, or porous materials impregnated with liquid or gelatin-like substances. This is typically used for recycling graywater as higher-quality water for cleaning, toilet flushing, industrial and cooling makeup water, and even drinking; for irrigation it is overkill.

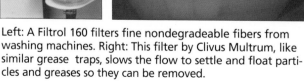

Left: A Filtrol 160 filters fine nondegradeable fibers from washing machines. Right: This filter by Clivus Multrum, like similar grease traps, slows the flow to settle and float particles and greases so they can be removed.

SOAPS, CLEANSERS, AND GRAYWATER

After water, the major component of graywater is soaps, detergents, bleaches, etc., followed by the oils, dirt, and grime that this water was used to remove.

• Soaps and salts

Soaps are alkali salts of long-chain fatty acids. They emulsify soils, microbes, and liquids, detaching them from surfaces and acting as a surface action agent (surfactant) to reduce the surface tension of water, making it "wetter." They break the bonds that hold these constituents to skin and fabrics, allowing them to be suspended in a form that can be rinsed away.

Most soaps are made with sodium hydroxide. The use of sodium-based soaps increases the sodium in graywater, while the hydroxide raises the pH, or alkalinity. Sodium can inhibit the water and nutrient transport in some plants' xylem and phloem cells by hindering the cell membrane's ability to transport water and nutrients, sometimes changing the osmotic balance. In other words, sodium causes hypertension in plants, just as it can in humans.

Potassium-based soaps are better to use with graywater-irrigation systems, because potassium is a fertilizer and a beneficial nutrient. Most liquid soaps are made with potassium hydroxide. Potassium hydroxide alone serves as an excellent grease remover; it works by turning grease into soap. Tripotassium phosphate is a powerful cleaner that is used on sewer pipes and automotive engines.

Soaps differ significantly from detergents in terms of how they perform. Hard soap and hard water can create tenacious soap scum. When using soft water (characterized by reduced calcium and magnesium ions) or naturally distilled rainwater, soaps may be preferable to detergents, because they are gentler and some say do a better cleaning job in soft water than detergents.

The gradual switch to detergent came when we started using hard water from wells and rivers, then found that hard soap left rings in bathtubs but detergents did not. Most hard soaps are made by reacting sodium hydroxide, a strong alkali, with clarified animal fat, lanolin, glycerin, or vegetable and citrus oils.

• Detergents and phosphatess

Shampoo, laundry and dishwasher powders, floor cleaners, face and body wash gels, and some toothpastes and mouthwashes contain detergents. Detergents contain surfactants, as well as chemicals such as: (l) "builders" that chelate (sequester) polyvalent metal ions such as calcium and magnesium ions that give "hard water" its name; (2) bleaches; (3) corrosion inhibitors; (4) sudsing modifiers; (5) fluorescent whitening agents; (6) enzymes; (7) antideposition agents; and (8) inert solid fillers (for texture). They penetrate wet soiled surfaces and displace, solubilize, or emulsify various substances, especially oils and greases. Before laundry detergents containing phosphates (mostly in anti-caking agents and builders) were banned by most states, graywater contributed one-half to two-thirds of the phosphorous in combined wastewater. Phosphorous can pollute surface water, but it is good for your garden.

• Degreasing cleaners

D-Limonene, a monoterpene, is the active ingredient in the mult-purpose concentrate cleaners that contain citrus oil derived from orange, grapefruit, and lemon extracts. It is is biodegradable and emulsifies oil, grease, tar, and cosmoline; it is noncorrosive and contains no petroleum solvents.

• Disinfectants and Antibacterials

Disinfectants can kill beneficial organisms as well as pathogens, although a robust constructed ecosystem should be able to withstand occasional small amounts of disinfectants, such as alcohol, chlorine or peroxide bleach, and antibiotics.

Due to growing concern over salmonella and E. coli bacteria contamination from beef and poultry operations, as well as "germs" in general, many cleaning and hygiene products now contain disinfectants. While this might be a scheme to sell products with fear-based marketing (disinfectants offer no major advantage over washing hands thoroughly with hot soapy water), it is a concern to operators of biological treatment systems. The overuse of disinfectants can reduce or upset the beneficial microbial populations both on our bodies and in our treatment systems. This is especially true with dishwashers in commercial kitchens which can discharge a lot of chlorine bleach used as a disinfectant. During the 1970s energy crisis, chlorine bleach was substituted for high-temperature water as a means to kill germs and reduce energy costs. This resulted in failed wastewater systems. With little or no biological processes in the treatment system, the fats, oils, and greases accumulate and clog the system. In the big picture, the increasing use of disinfectants allows resistant bacteria to morph into bacteria against which we have no antibiotics.

Diverting Urine

Every day, we flush away fertilizer in the form of urine. As much as 90 percent of the nitrogen (N) and half of the phosphorus (P) and potassium (K) in domestic wastewater is from the urine stream alone. These nutrients are the same fertilizing minerals purchased by farmers to grow crops. Urine is usually pathogen free, and it is in a liquid form that drains away easily (unlike feces

In one year, the average northern European adult produces 116 gallons of urine. An average daily nitrogen output for a healthy adult is about 11 grams but this varies widely. The more plant or animal protein the population eats, the more nitrogen it excretes.

In ecosystems, context is everything, so the fertilizer that is valuable for growing food on land is a pollutant (a resource in the wrong place) in the rivers and other waters where it is discharged as treated and untreated wastewater. In the aquatic ecosystem, it is too much of a good thing, resulting in proliferation of algae and

other plants. When these plants die, the decomposition process uses oxygen in the water needed by fish and other organisms.

In groundwater used for drinking water, nitrogen (as nitrates) might be a health risk, causing a low-oxygen blood condition called methemoglobinemia, although this is no longer considered a high risk.

As the effects of these nutrients become better known, wastewater treatment plants likely will be required to denitrify wastewater. This usually entails aerating wastewater to achieve the aerobic-anaerobic conditions that convert nitrogen to a gas form. Pushing air into large volumes of water requires a lot of power—all to remove the nutrients that gardeners, landscapers, foresters, and farmers purchase to grow plants.

Conventional wastewater treatment removes only a small fraction of the total nitrogen in wastewater: Only 1 to 3 percent of total nitrogen input is removed in the septic tank, with an estimated total removal of 21 to 25 percent when denitrification in the soil absorption system is included (Heufelder, 2006). In the northeastern U.S., the primary sources of the affecting anthropogenic nitrogen are atmospheric emissions (from vehicles and power generation), wastewater discharges, farms, and runoff. Among these sources, the single most easily diverted nitrogen source is human excreta, and specifically, human urine.

Before urine can be used for fertilizer, it must be oxidized to a form that plants can use called nitrate. Or it can be diluted and mixed into well-aerated soil, where the soil's aerobic microbes complete the oxidation (nitrification) process.

Using urine right away is best. If it is exposed to air for a while, the nitrogen starts to change into ammonia gas and waft away. (Nitrogen is an essential part of our atmosphere; it's what makes the sky blue.)

So how to isolate the urine stream? Swedish manufacturers started manufacturing toilets that divert urine to improve the ease of operating composting toilets, and Swedish researchers demonstrated the viability of using collected human urine to grow animal fodder crops.

To destroy pathogens that might be present in the urine, especially if it is from outside one's household, it should be stored for six months before use. This period

Clockwise from top left: A Duravit McDry waterless urinal, a urine-diverting flush toilet by Wost-Man Ecology (from top and side), and a Wost-Man DS waterless urine-diverting toilet

can be shortened if the ambient temperature is higher, such as 65°F. (Höglund, 2001)

The urea in urine is degraded into ammonia and carbon dioxide in storage (Vinnerås et al., 1999). This process raises the pH of urine from about 7 to over 9. This, combined with its high ammonia content, destroys any pathogens present.

For lowest risk usage, apply it to crops that do not touch the earth, such as orchard fruit, vines, and berry bushes. Or use it only for crops that will be cooked or fed to animals. When in doubt, don't use it.

Household urine can be used for growing food can be used without containment if one month is allowed to pass between application of the urine-fertilizer and harvest of the crop. (Schönning & Stenström, 2004)

One study found that diverting even half a community's urine enabled a wastewater treatment plant to work more efficiently and its biogas digester to produce three times more methane for power. (Wilsenach, 2006)

How to Keep It Separate

The easiest way to divert urine is with flush and waterless urinals. For women, urine-diverting toilets feature a cast-in urine drain. At least three European companies manufacture flushable urine-diverting toilets. Urine is flushed with about half a cup (0.1 liters) of water each use. Solids are flushed with .7 to 1.3 gallons (3 to 5 liters) of water to septic tank, sewer, or other system. Waterless urine-diverting toilets are also available for use with composters and drying toilets.

What to do with diverted urine:

- Collect, store, and pump it for application to hayfields, woodlots, and biofuel crops.

- Drain it to engineered urine-growaway gardens. (This works best with some dilution, such as with flushing water or graywater).

- Collect it for addition to local or community composting. (Most municipal wood chip composting requires some nitrogen).

With some communities now deemed nitrogen-sensitive zones requiring installation of costly denitrification systems to reduce nitrogen outputs by half, urine diversion offers economics and efficiencies too good to ignore.

Urine is applied to a field with a liquid fertilizer application apparatus before planting.

References

Höglund C. "Evaluation of Microbial Health Risks Associated with the Reuse of Source-Separated Human Urine." PhD thesis. Stockholm: KTH. 2001

Schönning, C. & Stenström, T.A. *Guidelines for the Safe Use of Urine and Faeces in Ecological Sanitation Systems.* EcoSanRes Publication Series. Report 2004-1. Stockholm Environment Institute:Stockholm, Sweden. 2004

Vinnerås, Björn, Jönsson Håkan. *Urine separation– Swedish Experiences.* 1999

Heufelder, George. Barnstable County, Massachusetts wastewater regulator. Personal communication. 2006

Wilsenach, Jac and Mark van Loosdrecht. Integration of Processes to Treat Wastewater and Source-Separated Urine. Journal of Environmental Engineering, vol. 132.

Sludge

Generally, sludge is a semi-solid settled from liquids from any number of processes. The main content of sludge is bio-available carbonaceous compounds.

Sludge from municipal wastewater treatment systems consists mainly of large solids screened out early in the process (primary sludge) and solids that did not liquefy or further break down during the treatment process, as well as dead cell bodies from the bacteria that treat wastewater (secondary sludge).

Sludge is potentially harmful if not properly managed. State and federal governments regulate how it can be processed and used or disposed. The reason is simple: Think about all that is flushed down toilets and drained from sinks and what is discharged by factories and other industries. In addition, pharmaceuticals used for depression, erectile dysfunction, birth control, and the like pass through bodies and appear in wastewater. Much of the chemicals, pharmaceuticals, and some disease-causing bacteria and viruses wind up concentrated in the sludge after most of the water has been removed.

Sometimes metals and polymers are added to improve settling by sticking to particles so they sink.

The management of sludge in wastewater treatment systems, including many of the ecological systems, is primarily accomplished with aerobic processing. Large amounts of electricity is used to blow in oxygen that supports aerobic (oxygen-using) bacteria. These bacteria rapidly consume organic matter and convert it into carbon dioxide. Once there is a lack of organic matter, bacteria die and are used as food by other bacteria. The objective is to convert the carbon to carbon dioxide (CO_2) to reduce the total volume of sludge for disposal. The increasing cost of electricity is causing designers to rethink this. Also, some anaerobic bacteria (for example, pseudomonas and dehalococcoides) are known to break down persistent organic compounds, including polychlorinated biphenyls (PCBs).

In some systems, called methane digesters, an anaerobic treatment process digests bioavailable carbon and converts it to natural gas (methane or CH4) before the solids are fully settled out as sludge.

Municipal and industrial wastewater plants spend millions of dollars disposing of sludge, either burning it, landfilling it, applying it to hayfields and forests, or using it as fill and landfill-capping material. In recent years, it has been sold as a fertilizer, either dried and pelletized or composted. To improve its acceptance, wastewater industry interests renamed it "biosolids." Although any pathogens in it likely have been destroyed, sludge's content of heavy metals, chemicals, and pharmaceuticals is a red flag to many. There is much controversy about the safety of allowing sludge, which might contain unknown and uncontrolled chemicals, to enter the food chain or the air via incineration. Federal limits on heavy metals and chemicals in sludge have driven wastewater facilities to control what industries discharge to municipal treatment plants. Many industries now have their own treatment systems. Or, their more toxic discharges are trucked away to hazardous waste facilities. Still, given the chemical cleansers and pharmaceuticals discharged by households daily, sludge reminds us we are all potential polluters who must be mindful of our choices and the destination of what we discard. At the same time, it underlines the value of keeping solids—excreta, toilet paper, and food wastes—separate so they can be composted and used with more security.

In New Paltz, N.Y., a constructed reed bed planted with phragmites helps dewater and reduce the volume of sludge to be disposed. (Photo: Jordan Valdina)

Biogas Digesters

Biogas plants, also known as anaerobic digesters and biodigesters, use anaerobic decomposition to produce CH_4 (methane), which can be used as an energy source. Methane can be produced with sewage sludge and even food, leaf and yard litter, and carbonaceous solid waste (paper and cardboard).

The rising price of energy necessitates considering this alternative source of energy. Many large treatment plants and landfills collect methane and burn it or use it to offset treatment costs. Some produce enough to supply municipal buildings and local neighborhoods with either gas or gas-generated electricity.

A biogas digester coupled with an engine and generator can burn biogas to produce combined heat and power (CHP). The heat from burning the biogas (CH_4 and CO_2) can be captured and used to preheat domestic hot water, reducing fuel needs or to provide higher quality heat for other purposes. An engine shaft drives a generator that provides electric power.

To provide significant volumes of gas, the digestion process needs more carbon than most wastewater readily offers. Shredded paper trash, waste vegetable oil, and even construction waste can easily provide the necessary carbon.

The disadvantage of methane digestion is the sometimes long period required for the process (up to 30 days) and the high capital cost.

Generally in a two-stage biogas digester, the carbonaceous solids are fermented to produce the liquid organic acid feedstock (such as acetic acid, $C_2H_4O_2$) for methane-producing microbes in the second stage. The second stage is a fixed-film reactor in which methane-producing microbes digest the organic acids produced in the primary reactor and produce biogas (CH_4 and CO_2).

An engine that burns biogas can be combined with an electric generator to produce combined heat and power. The engine can be either a microgas turbine, Stirling external combustion engine, or a standard diesel motor.

Biogas is composed of 50 to 70 percent methane, 30 to 40 percent carbon dioxide (CO_2), and low amounts of hydrogen, nitrogen, and water vapor.

Biogas is about 20 percent lighter than air and has an ignition temperature of 650° to 750°F. It is an odorless and colorless gas that burns with a flame similar to that of liquefied petroleum gas.

The production of CH_4 from wastewater does not diminish the nutrient values of the wastewater, so the remaining liquid, or supernatant, can be used to grow crops. During the digestion process, most if not all pathogens are destroyed.

Methanogenic bacteria develop slowly and are sensitive to sudden changes in physical and chemical conditions. A sudden drop in temperature by even a few degrees might significantly slow their growth and gas production rate. The process works best when it is kept warm.

Due to the challenge of managing these sensitivities and an even slurry consistency, as well as the need for a higher carbon-to-nitrogen ratio (about 30 to 1) than most wastewater offers, biogas digesters are usually used at very small scales, such as a tiny digester that supplies a flame for cooking in a developing country, and at large scales, such as for communities and large animal production operations where they power whole buildings and neighborhoods. Rarely are they found in use in single buildings. As the cost of imported natural gas and other fuels continues to rise, the economics of wastewater-derived methane will improve, and more technologies will appear on the market.

Boston's wastewater treatment facility includes 12 anaerobic digesters producing methane that helps power the plant.

Composting Toilet Systems

Blackwater can be composted into a stable end-product that need not go to a wastewater treatment plant.

The trick is to keep it as aerobic as possible by keeping it separate from the rest of the wastewater flow, dewatering it, and using microflush or flushless toilets. This can be accomplished with a composting toilet system.

A composting toilet (also known as a dry, biological, or waterless toilet) is an aerobic, unsaturated (not immersed in water) system that can oxidize and decompose excreta and toilet paper to as little as 10 percent of its original volume. It uses aerobic bacteria (those that use oxygen), which are more efficient than the anaerobic bacteria (which do not use much, if any, oxygen) at work in a septic system. The end-product is humus, which looks like soil, not sewage, and in many states legally can be buried under 6 to 12 inches of soil.

The term composting toilet is misleading. A composting toilet is actually a container composter, not just a toilet, which is simply a means of collecting and moving excreta and toilet paper to someplace else. A better term would be aerobic blackwater biofilter. A composting toilet does what a treatment plant would for septage and sewage and in fact might be more thorough. Because most of the pathogen count in wastewater is from the blackwater, keeping blackwater separate allows installing a graywater-only leachfield 35 to 40 percent smaller than a full-sized one in many states.

Many composting toilets grew out of designs for Scandinavian vacation cottages. Most are seen in parks, cottages, and environmental centers where there is no septic system or sewer service. Increasingly, they are showing up in year-round homes on environmentally sensitive sites.

The challenge is getting air to the composting process while minimizing human exposure to it. Composting toilets are comprised of (1) a waterless, microflush, or urine-diverting toilet, or a toilet opening on the composter itself, (2) an air intake, (3) an exhaust chimney, often with fan assist, (4) sometimes an internal means

Left: An under-floor composting toilet.
Right: A self-contained composting toilet.

of aerating, such as with a crank, grate, hanging net, or batching, and (5) leachate (liquid) drainage. Some systems have heaters to evaporate urine.

Because their contents are crumbly and dry and therefore not removed with a septage pump, these systems are above ground, unlike septic tanks. This has limited their adoption and acceptance.

Composting toilet systems range from little three-gallon composters for boats to large multicompartment systems that serve more than 100 users daily. There are several types of composting toilets:

• **Self-contained vs. Below-Floor Systems:** With self-contained systems, the toilet seat and a small composter container are all one unit. These can sit in the bathroom. Due to their small size, these are typically used in cottages and seasonal homes.

In a central system (also known as remote and below-floor), the toilet drains to a composter beneath the floor or in a basement or separate structure. They are the choice for high-capacity applications and facilities with multiple toilets.

• **Batch vs. Continuous Processing:** Every composting system uses either a single-chamber continuous composter or multichamber batch composter. A continuous composter features a single chamber into which excrement is continually deposited at the top, and finished compost is removed from the other end of the unit through a hatch or drawer.

Batch composters utilize two or more interchangeable composters; one is filled at a time, then allowed to completely compost while another composter fills. The advantage of batch composting is that advanced compost is not contaminated by fresh waste. Also, in some systems, the composter containers can be removed from the toilet to take outside to empty.

Larger units have long-term retention (two years or more), allowing longer composting periods and more capacity. The self-contained smaller systems are lower priced but require more frequent emptying.

You can purchase a manufactured composting toilet system or construct a site-built composting toilet system. The three most common types of site-built designs are twin-bin (or two-vault) systems, alternating drum (or roll-away trash bin) systems, and an inclined-vault system.

Maintaining Composting Toilet Systems

Composting toilet systems require periodic maintenance. Service contracts are available from some manufacturers and septage haulers.

The success of composting generally depends on four factors:

• **Heat:** Composting is most efficient at temperatures of 65°F to 135°F—the higher the temperature, the faster the composting.

• **Aeration and mixing** to get oxygen to the contents. Adding chunky carbon material helps keep the contents porous and more aerobic.

• **Microorganisms:** Composting is carried out by bacteria and fungi. Innoculate the composter with purchased microbes or a shovelful of finished compost.

• **Moisture:** Microorganisms need moisture to do their work, preferably within the range of 40 to 70 percent, with the optimum being about 60 percent (about the texture of a well-wrung sponge).

• **Carbon-to-nitrogen ratio (C:N) and additive:** For the composting microbes to fully transform the high-nitrogen content of excrement (mostly from the urine) to compost, it needs a carbon-to-nitrogen ratio of about 30 parts of carbon for one part nitrogen. However, because most of the nitrogen trickles down to the bottom of the composter, the C:N ratio of most of the content is sufficient.

• **Management:** As with all wastewater treatment systems, management is critical to the efficiency of the system. You've got to monitor levels and remove material every two years.

Odors and flies are feared byproducts of composting toilet systems. Closed designs and well-designed ventilation can avoid these problems.

Some systems divert urine to reduce the possibility of odors. In some urine-diverting toilet system designs use ash or lime additives; these are drying toilets designed to thwart biology, in contrast to the active biology promoted in a composting toilet.

Pathogens

Pathogens are destroyed in composting toilets in the following ways:

• **Antibiosis and pH:** Microbial and other higher order aerobic organisms develop in the compost pile during decomposition, creating antibiotics that kill pathogens. The alkalinity of compost is not suited to some pathogens.

• **Time:** Out of their hosts and favored environments, pathogenic microorganisms often die.

• **Predation:** Bacteria and fungi prey on some organisms and viruses.

Hot, or thermophilic, composting rarely occurs in contained composting, so heat is not a factor in pathogen reduction in these systems.

What to Do with the End-Product

Most states require transporting the end-product removed from a composting toilet to a treatment facility or burying it under at least 12 inches of soil, preferably within the root zones of nonedible plants that can use the nutrients. Many put the end-product in an outside composter for secondary composting. Although many owners use their composting toilet end-product on their food crops, this will not be supported by municipal health agents.

The leachate or liquid drained from composters can be removed or drained to a gravel-filled planter bed, with or without graywater. In fact, leachate can add needed nutrients to some graywater systems.

A Composting Future?

Composting toilets are fast losing their image as rustic toilets that are one step up from pit latrines. They are getting more serious attention from regulators, public health officials, and property owners thanks to the advantages of diverting blackwater and processing it aerobically to keep pathogens and nutrients away from where they can cause trouble. Increasingly, composting toilet systems will be serviced by central management districts, and the end-product taken to a central composting facility.

Turning blackwater into a stable, usable product before it is mixed with toxic chemicals and other materials that render it "pollution" is an increasingly appealing prospect to the resource management field. The septic tank of the future might be far less "septic" and more like its oxygen-using cousin, the composting toilet.

Mechanical Wastewater Recycling

One might say that all water on this planet is "reused," but today, the term water reuse describes the growing practice of treating and using wastewater to offset potable (drinking quality) water demand for nonpotable purposes such as irrigation, flushing toilets, and recharge of ground and surface waters. Treating wastewater to various qualities for various uses is occurring at all scales, ranging from a city's wastewater to household washing machine flows.

The driver for using this resource rich in water, nutrients, and organics is typically drought, notably in Australia, and the cost of meeting new water demands in growing American desert communities such as Los Angeles and Las Vegas.

Recycling Wastewater for Drinking

Where water is scarce or expensive, such as in Africa and parts of Asia, full wastewater recycling for potable use is increasingly practiced. Indeed, the ideal goal of many is to recycle all wastewater produced by a building and cycle it back for everything from washing to drinking. This approach, sometimes termed "toilet to tap" by its detractors, is not cost-effective for everyone. Three main challenges are regulations requiring a high standard of treatment, the high cost of both advanced filtration and piping water back to the point of use, and poor public perception. The city of San Diego, for example, encountered local protest to augmenting its water supply with recycled wastewater due to a perceived pathogen risk, despite the intensive treatment and disinfection of recycled wastewater.

Buildings are employing membrane bioreactors and reverse osmosis to treat wastewater before it is disinfected. But pushing wastewater through 1.0- to 0.5-micron membranes takes a lot of energy and requires operators. Another cost, if the water is deemed nonpotable, is the extra piping to supply water to other fixtures. This is called a dual-reticulation system.

Increasingly employed for wastewater reuse is membrane filtration. Membranes are hollow tubes or sheets of semipervious polymers with multiple microscopic holes sized to separate water from particles and pathogens. Wastewater is sucked through the membranes by pumps. The membranes provide ultrafiltra-tion, with a pore size of 0.2 micron. For potable use, this filtration is usually followed by ultraviolet (UV) or chlorine disinfection.

Also increasingly used are membrane bioreactors (MBR). This is membrane filtration integrated into a biological reactor that degrades particulates and destroys a high percentage of pathogens via traditional suspended-growth aerobic decomposition where some kind of media, usually plastic shapes, provides surfaces on which biofilms attach and transform the wastewater constituents. This reduces the wastewater components that must be filtered by the membrane. Again, pushing water through small pores requires a lot of energy. It also requires energy to backwash these membranes to remove the sludge.

There are other types of filtration used to convert wastewater to drinking water. The high cost of mechanically removing all unwanteds from this flow points to the value of instead using low-strength flows such as graywater and stormwater, which carry far less of a pathogen challenge and can be filtered with ultra-filtration (0.1 to 0.01-micron) after filtration by courser media filters such as sand-and-anthracite filters.

The same method is used for desalinization (also known as desalination), which removes salt from saltwater, although the typical method is to evaporate the water then capture it (distillation) minus the salts and minerals. Enormous amounts of power are needed to do this.

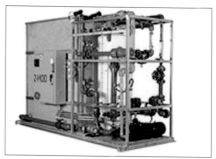

The Zenon reverse osmosis filter is one example of a membrane filter system.

Recycling Wastewater for Other Uses

Given the high expense and other issues associated with recycling wastewater for drinking, it is worth looking at the multitude of other uses that do not require such advanced treatment. Irrigation is the first, as it accounts for the largest use of fresh water in the United States and can use wastewater's nutrients. Groundwater recharge is another.

The slow acceptance is due to federal and state regulators' reluctance to approve any use unless the wastewater is treated to near drinking water quality. Pathogen count (total coliform and fecal coliform) and clarity are the main measures of quality for recycled wastewater. However, expensive sampling and testing push the cost for reclaimed water to levels that only the wealthiest communities can afford. At the same time, government agencies take the no-risk approach of requiring zero content of fecal coliform for even urban reuse and irrigation of landscapes and farm lands, in spite of epidemiological studies that show some presence of coliform is safe (highly unlikely to cause disease).

In the U.S., standards are established by individual states and sometimes local communities, with varying regulations and requirements. California has the strictest requirement of less than 2.2 total coliform bacteria/100 ml for irrigation of food crops (to be achieved through secondary treatment followed by filtration and disinfection) and less than 23 total coliform bacteria/100 ml for irrigation of pasture and landscaped areas (through secondary treatment and disinfection). (USEPA 625/R-04/108 Guidelines for Water Reuse, 2004)

The various approaches for wastewater treatment for reuse have sparked an international controversy. In 1989, the World Health Organization (WHO) published its guidelines for reuse for irrigating agriculture. It recognized that if the cost of treatment was too high, the water and nutrients would not be available to most of the world's population, only the ones that can afford the staggering cost of reverse osmosis and disinfection. The WHO settled on a quantitative microbial risk assessment (QMRA) model to generate an estimated annual risk of infection. This standard takes into consideration who is exposed to the effluent and their risk of contacting disease from the effluent. (1106 Bulletin of the World Health Organization, 2000, 78 (9)). After much debate, the WHO required 10/100ml[3]

of fecal coliform for unrestricted irrigation. This ensures that reclaimed water can be safely and affordably used by poorer populations that cannot afford American no-risk measures. Treatment possibilities for this quality includes retention in aerated lagoons and constructed wetlands.

Water Quality Standards

Table 2 in the Appendix is a summary of water quality parameters for conservative standards for unrestricted water reuse. The National Sanitation Foundation (NSF) is developing a comprehensive performance standard for manufacturers of recycling technologies so that they can offer new equipment for both wastewater and rainwater reuse. This will allow regulatory agencies to approve ANSI/NSF certified reuse technologies for building use as opposed to waiting for their city or state to furnish reclaimed water to their building.

Effective Reuse

The key to effective water reuse is to match the quality and quantity of the treated effluent with the desired end-uses. Seasonal issues dominate irrigation applications and some urban reuse applications in climates that routinely freeze in the winter. More water is needed in hot and dry environments. Raw or untreated wastewater, while rich in nutrients, contains a wide spectrum of human disease organisms, chemicals, pharmaceuticals, organics, minerals and solids that can make reuse irresponsible. Drawing attention to this problem is recent epidemic illness in the U.S. from vegetables rinsed in water drawn from sources contaminated by farm animal excrement.

Reused water is rapidly becoming a necessary addition to the water supplies of all countries. Droughts, population growth, and the increasing cost of treatment and delivery of natural water supply are the drivers. The nutrients and water in wastewater are too valuable to waste.

Reference

USEPA 625/R-04/108 Guidelines for Water Reuse, September 2004. This document identifies requirements for reuse for every U.S. state in the United States and is a valuable guide for communities and individuals interested in water reuse.

WATER RESOURCING

All of us drink water that is recycled and resourced every day.

The idea of drinking water that even a month earlier was discharged to a sewer pipe is often the deathblow to proposed wastewater-recycling schemes, despite extensive testing and controls that assure it is pathogen free and fit for drinking, sometimes far more than commonly used water sources. The public's aversion to anything that once had contact with human excretions and secretions was developed and perhaps overdeveloped by the association of excreta with illness.

There is no new water on this planet. All the water that is here is all that has ever existed. It is not created anew. It is not a renewable resource. We can only manage well the water we have. It continually enters and leaves living and nonliving systems in both aqueous and gaseous forms. At times, it is sequestered for eons in the ground or in ice. Water permeates every cell of our bodies and the ecosystems that sustain us. It is the majority ingredient of blood. As with blood, it carries needed resources to points of use, and it carries away "wastes" that, ideally, serve as resources for other organisms.

Water cycles through bodies, plants, soil, atmosphere, underground rivers, glaciers, oceans, and rain.

The water molecules you drank or bathed with today might have once been the amniotic fluid in which you were gestated or the blood of Moses, Jesus, Mohammed, Buddha, your friends, and your ancestors. And those molecules might one day feed your great-grandchildren or quench your thirst 50 years from now.

A rose by any other irrigation would smell as sweet: Graywater irrigates roses at the home of San Francisco TV news anchor Wendy Tokuda. (Photo: Mikka Tokuda Hall)

4. Integrated Strategies

"Water Crisis": Lack of Supply—or Strategy?

Emerging Approaches for Sustainable Water Management

As the world's population increases, migrates to the coasts, and builds new cities, urban planners are confronted with seemingly insufficient supplies of fresh water to meet the increasing demands.

This problem is not limited to arid zones. It is a function of population explosions and the inability to manage demand. "Even in water-rich countries such as Canada, lack of quality control for drinking water has led to death and illness in several communities, and some provinces suffer chronic shortages of water for agriculture; and almost everywhere capital costs for infrastructures to supply and remove water are growing." (Brooks, 2003).

Problems with the Current Approach

Most forecasted urban water crises are based not so much on the availability of water but on our failure to manage how it is used. At the root of the problem is the failure of urban planners to:

- Recognize stormwater as a resource
- View industry and cities as small watersheds onto themselves with various intakes and outflows of nutrients, organics, and water
- Start at the source when managing water and wastewater
- Reduce the use of water to transport wastes

Addressing urban water supplies is quickly becoming a high priority. The United Nations Population Fund estimates that by 2025, 61 percent of the world's population of 800 billion will live in cities (United Nations, 2003), creating population densities never before seen.

The problem is exacerbated as urban development follows the Western model of big pipes bringing fresh water from long distances to where it is used imprudently, then treating wastewater and discharging it into streams, lakes, and oceans. Or it flows to sophisticated expensive recycling treatment plants from which it is then distributed through more big pipes to where the water was wasted in the first place.

Continuing this model, urban planners will have to:

- Seek new supplies from other aquifers and surface waters. Yet these resources are already overtaxed in many areas and might rob water from outlying areas and agriculture.
- Desalinize seawater, which is very energy intensive.
- Recycle wastewater, which is also energy and infrastructure intensive.

> **Problems cannot be solved at the same level of awareness that created them.**
> **–Albert Einstein**

Recycling Is Not Enough

Arid regions are increasingly looking to wastewater recycling as the answer. While recycling wastewater is an important step in the conservation of fresh water, it is technologically complex, expensive, and unacceptable to many communities. It is expensive and energy intensive to remove vast amounts of minute particles and bacteria from enormous volumes of wastewater so that it is safe for direct human contact.

To identify advanced wastewater recycling and desalinization as the best answer to the world's water supply challenges is to use the same mentality that created today's many water problems.

The practice of centrally collecting combined effluents—including excreta, toxics, and heavy metals—from a wide variety of sources and then treating them with end-of-pipe solutions with advanced ultrafiltration will not be feasible for many cities, especially those in developing countries. This approach has evolved to avoid the complexity of using many smaller, more local, and effluent-specific strategies. Yet nature's model shows us that local complexity is the best way to manage resources.

It is clear that wastewater recycling will be a necessary strategy in the years ahead, but it is only one component of an ecological integrated water management program that offers economic benefits and treatment efficiencies. Such a strategy keeps water local by making best use of local sources of water and local effluents that can be recycled, as well as local sites. And although this strategy decentralizes water collection, use, and treatment, it still benefits from central management.

It requires us to heed the new tenet in water management: "Start at the source." By first seeking more local opportunities at the site of water use and wastewater production and according to what exactly is discharged, we can find possibilities for reducing water demand and treating effluents in more ecologically effective ways.

The QWERTY Syndrome

We humans have a curious tendency to continue old practices into the future long after the need for such practices has passed. Take the example of typing keyboards. The upper left row of letters begins with the letters QWERTY. This arrangement was developed in 1872 to slow down typists; otherwise the keys would jam on the early mechanical typewriters. We no longer have mechanical typewriters, yet we continue to use the old keyboard configurations to this day. It might be that this QWERTY syndrome is the root cause of some of today's most fundamental water-management problems.

QWERTY-type water management issues persist to this day:

• **Stormwater:** We must reverse the attitude that stormwater is not a resource but a pollutant we must quickly pipe away.

• **Linking water and sanitation:** One of the main impediments to sustainable water management is the historic linkage of water and sanitation. We must uncouple the use of potable water from sanitation as much as possible or forever be trapped in flushing away unwanted residuals, valuable organics, and nutrients (found in urine), as well as pathogens, with large volumes of water.

The Fundamental Problem

Essentially, we are using a valuable resource—drinking water treated and delivered at significant expense—to dilute and dispose of another potentially valuable resource, human excreta. To this we add industrial and household chemicals and stormwater. Then we pay a high price to transport this combined effluent to a facility that attempts to separate those constituents, clean them to a degree mandated by national law, and discharge the remaining water back into the environment, usually rivers, oceans, and the ground. In most cases, the same nutrients and toxic chemicals that went into the wastewater mix are still present in what leaves the treatment plant.

ADVANTAGES OF DECENTRALIZED ONSITE WASTEWATER RECYCLING

A water and wastewater plan composed of start-at-the-source reuse solutions offers the potential of a paradigm shift to watertight community-scale wastewater service delivery with the accompanying benefits of:

- No infiltration of stormwater into the pipes
- No exfiltration of sewage out of the pipes
- Pipes one-sixth the size of conventional pipes, because they do not accommodate stormwater
- No sewer overflow valves so no sewer over-flows to waterways
- No pumping stations
- No ocean or river outfalls for these systems
- No sewage bypassing the treatment plant in wet weather
- Rehabilitation of river and estuary aquatic ecosystems including fishing industries
- No long pipes traversing the countryside
- Flexible pipes that go around boulders, structures, trees, and cultural sites
- Small-diameter pipes that are relatively quick and cheap to install
- A range of local effluent-reuse opportuni-ties, including ones that can return money to the community
- Potential for integrated water management
- No chemicals used
- No byproducts sent to landfill
- Recovery of resources
- Closing the nutrient cycle
- Closing the water cycle
- Conserving water
- Reduced energy consumption and reduced greenhouse gas emissions, leading to the enhancement of our society on many lev-els—environmental, social, and economic

–Sarah West, Ph.D. "Innovative On-Site and Decentralised Sewage Treatment Reuse and Management Systems in Northern Europe and the USA," 2004.

Growing realization of the effects of this practice is prompting regulators to mandate fur-ther treatment—and that is making this com-bine-dilute-treat-and-dispose approach very expensive.

Every year we are learning more about the longer term effects of our present approach to cleaning wastewater: partial treatment and dis-posal. The 1972 Clean Water Act required the reduction of suspended solids, biological oxygen demand, and fecal coliform bacteria to protect lakes and rivers. Now, responsible regulators worldwide are mandating the removal of nutri-ents, toxic chemicals, parasites, viruses, radioac-tive wastes, and pharmaceuticals. At the same time, planners are asking: In a world where drinking water is increasingly expensive and scarce, can we use this valuable resource for flushing toilets?

It is clear that better ways are needed; the good news is that many are here and more are emerging. However, the answer is not merely a matter of more cleanup at the end of the sewage pipe. A larger, more strategic solution is needed, based on advanced water conservation;collec-tion, storage, and use of stormwater; on-site wastewater treatment; and recycling of water, organics, and nutrients.

Higher treatment costs and more regulations requiring better treatment are prompting a reframing of the wastewater management chal-lenge. With current practices, we create wastes we want disposed of. A better strategy is to put these to use just as they are in nature's model. In balanced ecosystems, there is no waste: The out-puts of one organism are the inputs of another.

Emerging ecologically oriented approaches for integrated water management reorient how we view the water and materials that flow through human communities. These approaches and their associated principles are urban and industrial watersheds and ecological sanitation.

Urban and Industrial Watersheds

Terrestrial life efficiently organizes itself around water and the mineral-rich land forms through which water flows. The life and all related activities within the water and land-form context is called a watershed.

A natural watershed synthesizes rainwater, solar energy, and minerals from within its physical, chemical, and biotic communities to produce an array of nutrients, raw materials, and products that sustain its inhabitants. The watershed comprises the surfaces upon which water falls (usually mountains and valleys) then drains into streams and rivers that flow to larger rivers, lakes, and oceans. Basins are where the water collects.

Typically, the watershed is viewed as the natural basins (often remote), rivers, or aqueducts around which human communities organize. However, human communities, including cities and industries, are both components of watersheds and are themselves watersheds. The urban and industrial watershed is defined by its rainwater, wastewater, and industrial process water flows and their interactions with each other and the surrounding watershed.

Usually, when we talk about using faraway watersheds to provide water, we talk about large basins and subbasins. The urban and industrial watershed zooms in further. Because most people soon will live in cities, these cities will be watershed basins unto themselves. Hardscapes—rooftops, buildings and their plumbing, and paved parking lots, streets, roads, and driveways—are the collectors or subbasins. When we think of human communities and their industries this way, and not as something apart from the natural watershed, we see a new universe of opportunities for managing and using water flows that do not require long-distance piping.

For example, some of the highest-quality water falls on rooftops. It is mostly uncontaminated and so needs only some filtration, storage, and possibly disinfection for use. Several countries, such as

Bermuda, rely on rainwater as a significant water source. Rain's potential contaminants are smog, dust, airborne contaminants, and any bird excreta on rooftops.

Stormwater is rainwater that has fallen onto surfaces and run off, collecting and dissolving pollutants and transporting them to nearby receiving waters. Water drained from paved surfaces is a far lower quality than water drained from rooftops due to the pollutants found on pavement: sediments, nutrients, trash, oil, grease, organics, pesticides, spills, vehicle emissions (fuels, lubricants, hydraulic fluids, oil, tire residues), road coatings, soot, animal and human excreta, intentionally disposed solids and liquids (such as used motor oil), and the list goes on. This stormwater runoff is a staggering volume of water, and cities typically let it drain away into rivers or sewers.

In several countries, stormwater is increasingly required to be cleaned or not discharged from the site at all. Federal and state governments are ratcheting down on the quality of stormwater that leaves a site. In the U.S., the recently enacted Phase II of the federal NPDES (National Pollutant Discharge Elimination System) requires communities and private developments to remove most of the pollutants in stormwater runoff that could affect water quality. Municipalities large and small now have to pretreat their stormwater, so it is coming to us at a quality better than ever before. It is now easy to collect and store with pretreatment for street washing, irrigation, fountains, and other nonpotable use.

Rainwater and stormwater, plus reclaimed wastewater, are sufficient in most cases to meet the demands of a community that practices water efficiency. Add to that other, cleaner flows such as condensate from cooling and refrigeration, and you have an effective integrated water management strategy.

Using rainwater can reduce water-supply infrastructure costs by displacing 80 percent of municipally supplied water. It is cheap to treat; the key is to invest in storage infrastructure. The rain comes at different times. Nature uses groundwater aquifers (veins of porous rock holding water) to store it. We need to use cisterns, in-ground and building-integrated tanks, and constructed aquifers. The best management practices required by NPDES slow down stormwater and detain it for a while, so it does not create floods or overload sewers. This detention requires tanks and basins. Collecting stormwater is already a mandate, so we might as well use it.

A Case of Untapped Liquid Assets

Consider the following example of an overlooked local water source in one of the world's largest cities: On average, New York City receives about 246,500 million gallons per year (937 Mm^3/yr) of stormwater, or 675 million gallons (2.57 Mm^3) per average day. (New York City has 836.1 km^2 of land area and receives 122.6 mm/yr of total precipitation.) While some is lost through evaporation, most is piped away into the adjacent rivers and out to sea.

New York City uses about 110 billion gallons per day (gpd) of city-supplied water, and that's after a municipal water-conservation program. According to the New York City Water Department, the city saved 400 million gallons daily of water by replacing old water-wasting toilets, installing locks on fire hydrants, and implementing a program to inspect underground water mains for leaks.

But the city can do more: If the stormwater had been collected, it would have satisfied 61.4 percent of the current demand. Using a 2006 New York City Water Department price of $3.94 per 100 ft^3 ($1.39 per m^3) for water service, the value of the stormwater is $3.56 million per day or $130 billion per year.

Stormwater could satisfy 100 percent of the city's demand if: (1) demand is reduced by an additional 22 percent by continued conservation and (2) recycled wastewater supplied 20 percent of the demand.

Yet the city draws its water from various watersheds in distant mountains, straining those communities around them and requiring miles of pipes.

New York City might instead look to capturing this stormwater, using some of the billions of dollars spent for collection and distribution pipe to fund cisterns, rooftop collection, and simple rainwater treatment to augment its water supply.

The key to future use of stormwater from urban and industrial watersheds is the commitment to investing in storage infrastructure. Stormwater, before it is piped away to mitigate flooding, should be stored to be available as an alternative water resource.

Integrated Water Management

The concept of urban and industrial watersheds should be part of the emerging goal of integrated water management. Increasing costs of water and wastewater treatment infrastructure are driving interest in integrated water management, which calls for combining stormwater infrastructure, integrating it with collected treated wastewater and water efficiency, and sometimes restoring natural systems. Currently, these services are managed by separate staffs in different places. This is still a disposal-oriented approach.

Water efficiency typically refers to conservation. In the U.S., water conservation is mandated for new buildings, with requirements for 1.6-gallon flush toilets and faucet aerators. In Australia, advances in water efficiency will grow as costs for supply, treatment, and delivery get higher and higher. In contrast, the term "effective" water management involves combining water flows to provide good performance as well as economic and ecological value.

Decentralization and Onsite Treatment

Another aspect of urban and industrial watersheds that also applies to rural settings is decentralizing wastewater management.

According to the U.S. Environmental

Protection Agency (USEPA) and the United States Census Bureau, onsite wastewater treatment systems are increasingly chosen over central sewer systems by property owners and municipalities, because they cost less than central wastewater treatment plants.

The most costly part of most urban wastewater systems is the piping and pumps to get wastewater to the treatment plant. That does not include the energy costs of pumping wastewater long distances. In California, an estimated 20 percent of the state's energy is used just to move water and wastewater to its destination. Decentralization avoids much of that cost while providing opportunities for using treated wastewater where it is needed.

Historically there has been a propensity to have large interconnected water basins connected by large pipes to large treatment systems then disposal to rivers and oceans. Engineers in communities thought it would be better to collect everything in one place and manage it with professionals, because they feared responsibility by local users was unfeasible. Today, the goal is to centrally manage decentralized systems throughout a community, so the best benefits of both decentralized and centralized approaches are put to work.

Decentralizing wastewater treatment can mean using a single system for each property or it can be a cluster or village-scale system at work for a group of buildings or neighborhood. One might call this approach distributed sewering.

Decentralization also offers better water security in the event of catastrophes and natural disasters. When the central treatment plant goes down, it goes down for a whole region. When water and wastewater treatment is decentralized, a calamity does not affect the entire region. If you are collecting rainwater and the municipal water supply goes down, you still have water supply.

Ecological Sanitation

In the late 1990s, some international development planners coined the term ecological sanitation, or "ecosan," to describe a more holistic, closed-loop approach to sanitation and wastewater management that emphasizes these main practices:

- Separation and containment of feces from the rest of wastewater flows for better treatment of this primary pathogen source and to minimize water pollution

- Reclaiminging nutrients (mostly from urine) as well as organics and water for use

- Minimizing or avoiding the use of water for toilet flushing

Ecological sanitation was used in developing countries where fecal-borne diseases were present and where limited water supplies made water-flush toilets unwise. As an approach, it recognizes that feces, which carry the highest potential for pathogen content, decompose more rapidly when kept separate from water and even urine, thus pathogens are destroyed faster. It also recognizes that urine contains the primary volume of nutrients in excreta, yet unlike the feces, has little to no pathogen content. Urine can be composted or applied to plants as a fertilizer. Many of its proponents are champions of waterless urine-diverting toilets; however, graywater-irrigation systems, composting toilets, constructed wetlands, and biogas digesters are also examples of ecological sanitation.

The Expensive Flush

Ecological sanitation avoids or minimizes the use of potable water to transport excreta, and so it emphasizes waterless and microflush toilets that drain to systems that manage only blackwater (toilet water). Many consider these options only for developing countries or remote buildings with no water or in very sensitive environments. But, as evidenced by the Choi Building at the

University of British Columbia in Canada, public buildings in Massachusetts, and a Swedish apartment building, waterless toilets are viable for even multistory buildings in relatively wealthy and water-rich countries. Besides reducing or eliminating the use of water for toilet flushing, these systems keep blackwater separate from other flows so it can be processed aerobically, a faster microbial transformation process. Excreta drops by gravity or is transported with foam via foam-flush toilets or small amounts of water with one-pint flush toilets or vacuum toilets. Some collect the blackwater in an intermediate tank until a sufficient volume accumulates to move with greater force through the pipes. Others use a small graywater "chaser" to scour pipes occasionally.

In current practice, these toilets drain to aerobic composters, so blackwater is processed onsite. They could also drain to an aerobic blackwater-only treatment system onsite or shared by nearby buildings. Increasingly, these systems are far more efficient, refined, and proven.

Every year, more states change laws and regulations to permit these toilets. Even researchers at Harvard University declared waterless recycling toilets to be the technology of the future and developed a high-tech prototype waterless blackwater system with solid-state sensors and microchips that control the process. By not mixing blackwater with graywater, the system stays more aerobic, reducing treatment time and avoiding the need to aerate the process.

Most microflush, vacuum-flush, and foam-flush toilets are installed to reduce overall wastewater volume and to save water. The forecasted "water crisis" calls on engineers and designers to perfect the technologies of waterless and microflush toilets with the addition of pipes and seals better suited to systems not scoured and sealed by water.

Another advantage: Graywater, a low-strength, nearly pathogen-free effluent, can be treated and used to irrigate plants in landscapes, planter beds,

SEWAGE MINING

Sewer mining is the process of tapping into a sewer line (either before or after the sewage treatment plant) and extracting sewage to be treated in a small on-site treatment plant for nearby use as recycled water. It is most economical for sites that use high volumes of water where water costs are high and where sewer lines or mains pass nearby. Industries and golf courses in arid regions are natural candidates.

Some sewage miners have used membrane reactors and package treatment plants to treat the wastewater. The treatment method depends mostly on the quality of water needed for its purpose. An engineering challenge would be to remove more water than sludge from the sewer line, so sludge does not have to be managed.

In Sydney, the sewage miner must hire a licensed water services manager and provide a very specific plan for how much, when, and how the sewage will be treated and distributed, as well as how remaining sludge will be managed.

The Sydney Olympic Park Authority's Water Reclamation and Management Scheme was Australia's first large-scale urban recycling scheme to use sewage mining to provide water for irrigation and residential nondrinking uses. Recycled water replaces 50 percent of the drinking water that would otherwise be used at the Sydney Olympic Park.

and greenhouses—and even recycled back to the building for use.

Using potable-quality water to flush toilets is a practice that will come under increasing scrutiny as cities grow. According to the USEPA, Americans use more water to flush toilets every day than they do to bathe and that drinking-quality water is expensive. For example, by the 2000 census, the population of New York City was 8.1 million. Assuming that the average person flushes a toilet 5.1 times per day (Vickers, 2001) and the average water use per flush is three gallons (11.36 liters), then New York City flushes about 123.75 million gallons—$650,000 worth—of drinking water into the sewers every day.

Financing Decentralized Systems

The USEPA and regulators worldwide are recommending the formation of management districts. These involve a central organization that manages and troubleshoots a district's onsite systems, so no matter what system a property owner uses, an agency would be accountable for its performance. The formation of these districts would allow onsite systems to receive federal funds for design, construction, and maintenance. These funds were previously provided only for central wastewater treatment plants. This same approach is increasingly used to manage decentralized stormwater systems as a stormwater utility.

More and more, incentives for diverting and using water flows within the city will be implemented by municipalities and perhaps fine-tuned by green building rating systems. New York City offers a 25 percent discounted water and sewer rate to property owners who install rainwater collection and wastewater-recycling equipment for onsite nonpotable reuse.

Incentives for water reuse and rainwater collection, such as tax credits, fast-track permitting, and development-density credits (allowing more building than zoning permits), will become common, as they are becoming for innovative stormwater management features. The city of Berlin in Germany requires all stormwater to be managed onsite and even prescribes the methods to accomplish that. Such mandates might extend to water and wastewater use. Currently, the city of San Diego requires proposed large developments to show where their

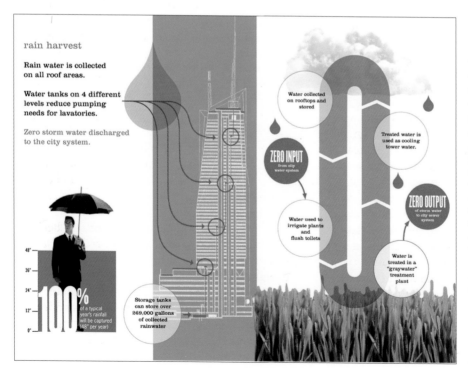

The Bank of America tower in New York City treats and uses its site's water flows–graywater, stormwater, rainwater, cooling coil condensate, and even basement seepage–to supply most of its water use. In turn, the city will charge Bank of America a lower water rate for the small volume of city-supplied water the tower uses. This is a reward for reducing demand on the city's increasingly taxed water supply. It's a good example of the urban and industrial watershed at work. (Graphic: Doyle Partners for Cook + Fox Architects)

water will come from. The city does not guarantee water supply to all new projects.

Big Pipe, Little Pipes: Two Scenarios

Compare and contrast the following scenarios.

• **Hypothetical big-pipe water-recycling scenario:** An urban neighborhood in New York City comprises industrial, residential, and commercial buildings. The water supply transferred from a distant watershed basin is now completely replaced with recycled water. Miles of pipes and pumping stations carry the wastewater to a treatment facility converted to a full water-recycling facility miles away. Stormwater is piped to rivers and out to sea. To supply recycled wastewater back to this neighborhood, pipes and pumping stations must be dug and installed, with great disruption to the city, to pipe water via the existing supply lines or new ones. Cost of the ultrafiltration and distribution is considerable.

• **Hypothetical integrated urban and industrial watershed water scenario:** The same New York City neighborhood is offered incentives to conserve and recycle water. Several buildings are retrofitted with low-water, dual-flush urine-diverting toilets flushed with treated graywater collected from sinks and showers. The flushed urine, which accounts for most of the nitrogen in wastewater, is used to fertilize and irrigate landscaping, green strips, parks, and green corridors via a subsurface piping system. Some urine is piped to greenhouses on industrial rooftops and brownfields to grow food, trees, or biofuels. Stormwater is collected from roofs, streets, and parking lots and treated and disinfected to be used for flushing toilets and urinals and for evaporative air conditioning.

Graywater and combined wastewater is treated onsite with a polyculture of treatment systems, including constructed ecosystems that double as landscaping, parks, gardens, bird habitat, arboretums, orchards, and even fountains. These systems create an incentive for planners to create green spaces, such as terraces and public gardens.

The beauty of these ecological designs increases land values and foot traffic in neighborhoods.

Toilet and kitchen effluent drains to treatment tanks for these appliances only. Septage is taken to a septage composting facility. Recipients of this composted septage (sludge) are relieved to know that no industrial chemicals, toxics, or heavy metals are in this material, unlike today's composted sewer sludge. Or, dry or microflush toilets drain to aerobic blackwater systems from which the end-product is periodically removed to a central processing facility.

Industrial flows with toxics and heavy metals are treated separately by systems designed for these specific constituents. Cooling water and condensate are recovered and recycled.

To minimize combined wastewater-stormwater sewer overflows, rooftops are retrofitted with green ecoroofs to absorb stormwater and evaporate it. Some of this water is drained to cisterns. These ecoroofs also reduce heat islands in the city, insulate buildings, and extend the life of roof membranes. Raingardens, pervious paving, and other lower-impact development techniques are used to infiltrate stormwater, reducing flows to the wastewater treatment plant.

Brownfields are used to infiltrate effluents and stormwater. Unused buildings might house storage tanks and treatment works. Marginal buildings can be dismantled to make way for collection, treatment, and planted treatment systems.

Some uses are seasonal. Rainwater can be used during wet months, and treated graywater used during dry months.

A city management team periodically checks the systems. This staff formerly worked in the central plant or is funded with savings from avoided central treatment costs.

The result: Much-reduced flow to the wastewater treatment plant and reduced demand for water. In addition, this scenario provides incentives for building users to reduce toxics and perhaps water usage.

Soft Path Water Planning

The holistic planning strategies described in this section are increasingly referred to as soft path water planning. It emphasizes complex systems approaches, versus a technology approach, to managing water.

While the hard path refers to infrastructure (pipes and pumps), soft path planning views water as a supplied service for use in sanitation, agriculture, etc. It employs demand management techniques, such as tiered pricing of water and incentives for efficiency, to use water more strategically. It also looks at diverse uses of water, matching water quality to the quality required by the use–especially in light of the fact that less than one third of water use requires drinking water quality.

Soft path planning emphasizes integration of municipal agencies, utilities, service providers, and stakeholders in water use and provision.

For a Secure Water Future

Centralized wastewater recycling will be a necessary strategy in the years ahead. However, it is only one component of an integrated water management plan that uses the integrated principles of urban and industrial watersheds and ecological sanitation. Such a strategy makes best use of local sites, local water sources, and local effluents that can be recycled.

To identify wastewater recycling and desalinization as the best solution to the world's water supply challenges is to use the same mentality that created today's many water problems. If the age of cheap petroleum and coal power wanes, it is clear that combining excreta, toxics, heavy metals, and many other constituents in a water-carriage wastewater infrastructure and then treating this soup with end-of-pipe solutions with advanced ultrafiltration will be not be feasible for cities in many developing countries and perhaps the developed world too. This approach evolved in an effort to avoid complexity. Yet ecosystems show us that complexity weaves a web of resiliency and multifunctionality that can withstand catastrophes, provide water to more users, avoid unnecessary energy losses, and provide water security in the 21st century as cities brimming with people must live with the same volume of water that has existed on this planet for thousands of years.

References

Brooks, D.B. "Another path not taken: A methodological exploration of water soft paths for Canada and elsewhere." Report to Environment Canada. Friends of the Earth Canada, Ottawa, Canada. 2003.

Del Porto, D. "Urban and Industrial Watersheds" in Water Crisis: Myth or Reality, Taylor & Francis Group, New York. 2006.

Del Porto, D. and Steinfeld, C. The Composting Toilet System Book. Ecowaters Books, Massachusetts. 2000

Del Porto, D. and The Ecological Engineering Group. Consulting Report for Ford Motor Company. Massachusetts. 2001.

New York City Department of Environmental Protection. "City Introduces Innovative New Comprehensive Water Re-Use Program." DEP News, [www.nyc.gov/html/dep/html/press/04-16pr.html].

United Nations. UN Report says world urban population of 3 billion expected to reach 5 billion by 2030. Press Release, POP/899. United Nations Population Division. [www.un.org/esa/population/publications/wup2003/pop899_English.doc]. New York, 2003.

United States Environmental Protection Agency, "Response to Congress on Use of Decentralized Wastewater Treatment Systems." USEPA Office of Wastewater Management, Washington, D.C. [www.epa.gov/owmitnet/mab/smcomm]. 1997.

Vickers, A. Handbook of Water Use and Conservation. Waterplow Press, Massachusetts. 2001

WateReuse Association. "WateReuse Association Testifies before Subcommittee on Water and Power." [www.watereuse.org]. 2003.

Australia, a Model for Integrated Water Strategy

In Australia, both the worst drought in 100 years and rapidly growing cities are driving a revolution in water use. The cities of Sydney, Melbourne, Victoria, and others are implementing integrated strategies for conservation and water harvest to avoid expensive drastic measures such as interbasin transfers, desalinization plants, and advanced water recycling.

Water demand has been reduced by about 47.5 billion gallons (180 billion liters) per year. Sydney, for example, now uses a comprehensive portfolio of measures to reduce potable water demand and diversify water supply:

- Rainwater collection for irrigation and washing: including rebates for installing tanks

- Graywater use: including rebates for graywater diversion fixtures and legal permission to use untreated graywater for irrigation

- Low-flush toilets and ultraconservation fixtures: A retrofit and rebate program

- A water-efficiency labeling for water-conserving fixtures and appliances, required for all fixtures sold

- A program to detect leaks and reduce water pressure to homes

- A water and energy efficiency building certification program (BASIX)

- A targeted "Every Drop Counts Business Program" to identify specific conservation measures in public buildings and businesses

- Tiered water pricing

- A Water Savings Fund that funds water-saving projects by businesses, communities, and others

- Water Savings Action Plans that require high-volume water users to develop plans that describe current water use and identify potential savings

- Outdoor water use and landscape assessment programs

- A public education program

- Sewage mining: Incentives for tapping into sewer lines to mine wastewater for treatment, then use

- Wastewater recycling: Incentives for fully treating wastewater for potable or nonpotable use

BASIX Water-Efficiency Certification

Introduced by the New South Wales government, BASIX (Building Sustainability Index) is a certification tool to reduce the drinking water demand and greenhouse gas emissions of new and renovated homes and apartments by setting energy- and water-reduction targets. It requires water-use reduction of about 40 percent of average household demand. All applications for new development or alterations to existing buildings must include a BASIX certificate, which is received by entering building design data in the BASIX Web site. If the design meets the water and energy targets, the user prints out a BASIX certificate. A certifying authority later visits the building to verify the measures are in place. BASIX requires a range of measures, such as water-efficient showerheads, dual-flush toilets, rainwater tanks, and graywater treatment systems. In the city of Melbourne, a similar program is called 5 Star Homes.

Source: "Review of the Metropolitan Water Plan: Final Report," Institute for Sustainable Futures, University of Technology, Sidney, Australia. April 2006.

The Green Paradigm
Can a source of clean energy be as close as the sewer pipe?

Wastewater offers a significant amount of energy that goes down the pipe every day.

Consider these opportunities:

• **Heat recovery:** Most sewage is 50° F (28°C), so capturing the heat from wastewater with heat exchangers makes sense. Heat can be captured to heat buildings, melt snow on roads, heat greenhouses growing winter food crops, and more.

• **Methane digestion:** Wastewater's carbon can be used to make methane (CH_4), or "biogas," to supply cooking gas, heat, electricity, vehicle fuel, and anything for which natural gas (from the ground) is used. In methane digestion, the only constitutents removed are Cs, Os, and Hs (carbon, oxygen, and hydrogen).

After heat is reclaimed and methane produced, wastewater's macronutrients (nitrogen, phosphorus, and potassium) are still intact and can be used to grow plants.

Green Energy

Wastewater's nutrients, organics, and water make it an ideal resource for growing plants. If those plants are not to be eaten, then the wastewater does not have to be treated to potable quality. Today's laws require cleaner discharges to lakes, rivers, and oceans, so this is another opportunity.

We can avoid upgrading to treatment plants to

In Sweden, a willow crop grown over three years with wastewater is harvested for a biomass-to-power facility. (Photo: Anja Brüll)

advanced tertiary treatment, if we instead direct wastewater treated to advanced primary or secondary standards to nearby barren lands to grow nonedible oil plants for refineries or cellulosic grains for ethanol. Instead of investing billions of dollars in wastewater pollution prevention and remediation, we can invest in the distribution system necessary to transport wastewater from existing treatment plants and animal feedlots to arid farmlands, deserts, and polluted brownfields to grow biologically based petroleum alternatives on land unfit for food crops. Because the nutrients and organics will be used by plants, they do not have to be treated.

This is the Green Paradigm™, a model that calls for using the resource productively instead of improving disposal.

Growing away our wastewater can reduce or eliminate the purchase of imported natural gas and petroleum within the next few growing seasons by growing oils, algae, and grains that can be processed to replace imported petroleum.

This vision is not new. The automaker Henry Ford invested heavily in soybean research, and before his death, manufactured a 1942 Ford concept car with most of its components made from materials produced by American farmers.

- Most petroleum-based chemicals, fuels, lubricants, plastics, pharmaceuticals, chemicals, and other products can be replaced by oils, grains, and biomass grown on American lands by experienced local farmers without significant changes in the refining, processing, and distribution systems now in place within the borders of the United States.
- Pollution from human- and animal-produced wastewater will require an investment of tens of billions of dollars in the next 10 years. The USEPA states that a trillion dollars were invested by American communities in the last 20 years to protect our water resources with upgraded water infrastructure. It is now estimated that another trillion dollars will need to be invested in the next 10 years.

- A preliminary estimate suggests that the wastewater from Reno and Las Vegas, Nevada, could produce more than 10 million barrels (420 million gallons) of palm oil per year. The wastewater would be pipelined to nearby barren lands instead of discarded in sensitive surface waters.
- The water and nutrients in human-derived wastewater in the United States alone can sustain more than 12 million acres of corn or 64 million acres of soybeans or rapeseed per year. This number can be doubled or tripled by adding poultry and other animal wastes to the equation.
- The nitrogen-rich gasses from American power plants can be used to grow millions of gallons of oil derived from the single-cell plant called algae instead of polluting the air, which results in billions of dollars in American productivity losses and health-related costs. These algae-oil facilities can be placed directly on power plant facilities, eliminating the need for transportation costs of fuel for the power plants.
- American farmers need new crops to replace tobacco and other crops that compete with foreign imports. Many farmers are still paid via U.S. government subsidies to not grow crops at all. Growing petroleum alternatives creates more jobs in areas where employment is needed without threatening existing farming communities.
- The U.S. could disconnect from the political liabilities of its fuel dependence on other countries.
- It takes 40 pounds of nitrogen fertilizer to grow an acre of legumes such as soybeans versus more than 200 pounds of nitrogen fertilizer for corn, because like most legumes, soybeans can fix nitrogen from the air and corn cannot. Therefore, oil-producing soybeans and the Pongam Bush (Pongamia Pinnata) are the preferred crop to use the nitrogen content of wastewater. However, the greatest oil production per acre is from the Oil Palm Tree, which would thrive in the southwestern deserts with adequate water and nutrients.
- One obstacle to growing petroleum alternatives is the cost of fertilizer, which requires natural

gas and petroleum to produce. The other is the lack of fertile land not already in service to growing food. By using wastewater and unusable land, these obstacles can be overcome. According to John Sawyer, associate professor of agronomy at Iowa State University, the majority of nitrogen fertilizer sold in the Midwest is either anhydrous ammonia or products made from anhydrous ammonia (urea, ammonium nitrate, and urea-ammonium nitrate solutions). Natural gas is a major component of ammonia production for both energy and supply of hydrogen (H) in ammonia (NH_3).

Therefore, the ammonia production cost is closely tied to the price of natural gas. Natural gas supplies derived in the U.S. are nearly depleted, so much is imported from other countries, such as Algeria and the Middle East. Natural gas accounts for more than 85 percent of the total ammonia production cost. When the price of natural gas increased in 2004, the cost of nitrogen fertilizer also increased dramatically.

• Tens of millions of acres of unusable land in America could be farmed to grow petroleum alternative crops with the water and nutrients in wastewater.

• American vehicles, including SUVs, can use fuels (biodiesel and alcohol) derived from vegetable oils and grains with only minor changes. This means there would be no need to penalize Americans for driving the vehicles they choose to drive. This averts the gasoline crises and lowers air pollution.

• The existing infrastructure of the petroleum industry (refineries, distribution, and chemical factories) can, with minor modifications, easily convert from petroleum to oils from soybeans and alcohols from grains.

Using the Green Paradigm to manage wastewater eliminates pollution of receiving waters, avoids the need to upgrade treatment plants to advanced secondary or tertiary standards and reduces dependence on imported fossil fuel.

What's more, in the big picture, growing away wastewater with plants and using energy from plants is sequestering carbon. Using current carbon instead of ancient carbon will slowly reduce the impact on global warming.

Modern Alchemy

Swedish Resourcefulness Turns Wastewater Into Heat and Energy

By Stephen Salter, P.E.

We are literally sitting on a huge source of renewable energy: our own excreta and the warm water we drain down the pipe every day.

While our politicians ponder a nuclear future, heat pumps can recover enough heat from our sewage to heat one-third of our buildings.

While oil companies drill for fossil fuels (the carbon of millions of years ago), we spend millions of dollars to bury millions of tons of organic energy in the form of sewage sludge and kitchen and plant waste in landfills every year—waste that could be transformed into biofuels.

Waste pollutes twice; first when it hits the environment, and again when we extract more resources to replace those we've discarded. Most people understand how recycling beverage cans reduces mining for metal. Now, we are beginning to understand recycling works with solid waste (garbage and trash), excreta, and wastewater, but we are far from effective when it comes to municipal waste and sewage. Landfills and sewage outfalls are dead ends—massive failures of imagination. In reality, the value of recycling the resources we waste is far greater than the value we receive by disposing of it.

For example, at current growth rates, the city of Victoria in Canada will outstrip its water supply in a few decades and perhaps sooner with climate change. When we drain the next water source, we will do permanent damage to a local river system. When we create waste, we waste creation. If instead we use rainwater more intelligently and reclaim water from sewage for irrigation, we can prevent that damage. This lesson has been learned in drier regions like Australia and California, where reclaimed water is sold for irrigation and to industry.

The author fills his car with biogas produced with wastewater from the city of Kristianstad. (Photos: Stephen Salter)

Putting Waste to Work

Sweden provides great examples of what the waste-free future can look like and serves as a model of cutting-edge best practice for the rest of the developed world.

The oil supply crisis of 1973 started Sweden on the road toward energy independence and recent drivers for using biofuels include climate change and a desire for cleaner air in cities. Interestingly, Sweden's carbon dioxide emissions have fallen by 4 percent since 1990 while Canada's have risen 24 percent.

Sweden has established a goal of using no petroleum-derived fuel by the year 2020.

Steering policies include a carbon tax on fossil fuel to reflect its real cost to the environment and to encourage use and production of renewable fuels such as biodiesel, ethanol, and biogas.

Particularly notable is Sweden's increasingly widespread use of wastewater methane digesters and wastewater heat recovery for municipal power and heating.

When organic waste decomposes in anaerobic digesters, it produces a mixture of methane and carbon dioxide. After the carbon dioxide is removed in an upgrading plant, the biogas is indistinguishable from natural gas.

Unlike the carbon in fossil fuels, the carbon in biogas is current carbon (not ancient underground carbon) pulled from the atmosphere by plant life and converted to food or landscape before it is excreted or harvested and put in the digester. You might say this is carbon sequestration. When biogas is burned, the carbon returns to the atmosphere, completing a cycle. Unlike the one-way trip of carbon from fossil fuels, biogas from waste does not contribute to climate change. Another benefit of biogas is that it produces fewer traditional pollutants like smog and less particulate emissions than fossil fuels.

Stockholm's Hendriksdals plant treats both sewage sludge and kitchen waste in its digesters to produce biogas for 50 buses with a goal to fuel 200 buses by 2010. Biogas from the plant also provides cooking fuel for the green development of Hammarby Sjöstad. Residents and restaurants deposit all food wastes (which are banned from Swedish landfills) to receptacles from which they shoot via underground vacuum tubes to a central collection point and on to the sewage plant to be co-digested with sewage sludge to produce more biogas.

Meanwhile, the heat in the wastewater is sold to the local energy company Fortum, where heat pumps extract enough energy to provide heat and hot water for 80,000 homes in Stockholm via district heating.

Hammarby Sjöstad, a neighborhood in Stockholm, features a scenic stormwater-collection canal.

This tertiary wastewater treatment plant is paid for by revenues from sales of biogas and heat, reducing the overall cost to below the Canadian average for basic secondary treatment.

In Gothenburg, financial and environmental benefits of wastewater-derived energy are compelling. In the 1970s, fossil fuels caused heavy smog in Gothenburg; the city responded by developing a district-heating network.

District heating costs less than oil or electrically generated heat. It also gives companies such as Gothenburg Energy an incentive to insulate their customers' buildings, which leaves more heat to supply to more subscribers. In this way the interests of Swedish energy companies and the environment are aligned. In North American energy firms, profit comes from selling more pollution, the result of selling energy as a commodity rather than as a service.

After heat is extracted from sewage, the water is just above freezing. Energy companies direct this "coolth" through a separate network of district cooling pipes to provide refrigeration and air conditioning to stores and offices.

Gothenburg Energy employs 1,000 people to provide renewable energy from waste. Sweden is proving that completing ecological cycles is not only better for the environment, but better for the economy.

At two meters below sea level, Kristianstad, a community of 35,000, is the lowest point in Sweden, and climate change is on the community's mind. Farm fields sprout wind turbines beside the crops. Agriculture and related food industries produce organic waste, which in 1995 the city decided to turn from a liability into an asset. The solution was to build the Karpalund biogas plant, which accepts waste from kitchens, food factories, and farms. In a great example of closed loops,

Food and yard wastes are deposited in chutes from which they are transported via vacuum to the methane digester.

farmers deliver manure to the Karpalund plant, then reload with the liquid residue from the digester. This residue, which is rich in nutrients and free of contaminants, is returned to farmland. The bulk of the solid residue from the methane plant digesters is composted separately for industrial landscaping.

In Kristianstad, biogas runs all of the community's transit and school buses, several city trucks, a dozen taxis, and about 200 cars. The surplus goes to a cogeneration plant that provides electricity and district heating. Biogas in Sweden is about 25 percent cheaper than gasoline, partly due to the Swedish carbon tax and partly because it comes from waste. Kristianstad encourages its citizens to separate their organic waste by charging more for mixed waste and encourages car owners to switch to biogas by subsidizing the cost of conversion and providing owners of biogas cars with free parking. These measures are part of the community's "fossil-free Kristianstad" initiative. Kristianstad stands as a leading example of the power of integrated resource and community planning.

Some might wonder if the practices in Sweden can work elsewhere, where costs of energy, environmental regulations, and tax structures differ. Swedes questioned about their views on their country's high taxes (relative to the United States) and the environment suggested that to them, knowing people and the environment were looked after means peace of mind, and so justifies their taxes. The Swedish law called "allemansrätt," (translated as "everyman's right" of common access) grants Swedes the right to traverse and even camp on private land, within simple guidelines concerning respect for owners' privacy and livelihood. The result is a stronger bond with the environment and a sense of the entire country being part of the public commons.

Beyond the social and environmental value of resource recovery, Sweden is showing how it is good for the economy. Biogas and district heating in Sweden are good examples of radical resource productivity, and the country is going further still by reducing taxes on employment and increasing taxes on raw materials, including fossil energy.

These Swedish cities make waste pay its own way by counting every output as an input, every

A biogas-fueled bus in Stockholm

waste as a resource. Recovering more value from waste costs less overall by reducing waste and pollution and producing energy and heat.

Waste Used for Highest Purpose

We need to use each resource for its highest and most direct purpose. It makes sense to save drinking water for drinking and reclaimed water for lawns. For example, until last year, the sewage treatment plant in Stockholm burned some of its biogas to heat its treatment processes. The plant now buys heat from the energy company, an exchange that makes more biogas available for city buses. The result is less pollution overall, higher economic returns for the treatment plant, and lower costs for the bus company.

More than a century ago John Muir said "When we try to pick out anything by itself, we find it attached to everything else in the universe." In North America, as organic waste rots in our landfills, it produces methane, a greenhouse gas with 21 times the global warming potential of carbon dioxide. The leachate from landfills pollutes our water. In contrast, when Swedes divert kitchen waste from landfills and into biogas digesters, this single change reduces

District heating pipes in Gothenburg

water pollution and greenhouse gases from landfills, reduces greenhouse gases from fossil fuels, reduces dependency on oil, and creates local employment.

Opportunities at Home

Our words for waste reflect our mindset and interfere with creative thinking. When we call sewage outfall an "effluent plume," it sounds elegant and innocent. A "landfill" sounds vaguely like an effort to heal the land. It's time to reorient our thinking, beginning with our language. The word resource means "to rise again," and if we talk about resource recovery rather than disposal, we begin on the path to optimal, ecologically healthy cycles.

We also fail to see our place in the ecosystem, preferring instead to put ourselves at the top of the food chain and above nature's laws. Our municipal governments work in silos and subcommittees, fragmented and missing the big picture. Departmental specialists in solid and liquid waste, transportation, and energy toil in isolation, because we do not hold our cities to

account for an ecological bottom line. Our administrations are designed to optimize administrative convenience, not environmental and social benefits. We have fragmented our governance, our academic institutions, our practitioners, our thinking, our resources, and our efforts.

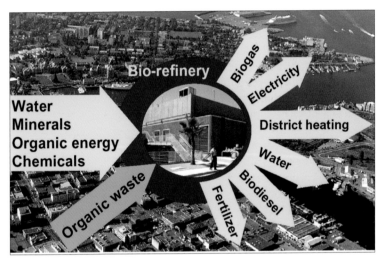

In several Swedish cities, wastewater is transformed into multiple resources.

Finally, the "yuck" factor comes into play, as we prefer to put our discharges, excretions, secretions, and effluvia away from us rather than see them as part of whole systems as most of our ancestors did. Our understanding of germ theory is now detailed, and we no longer need to flatly reject controlled handling of waste end-products.

Sweden is living proof that protecting the environment nurtures society, because thousands are employed there producing resources from waste. Why do we believe those who say curbing carbon will harm the economy? Who profits from the status quo, and who suffers?

Ultimately we are the architects of our communities. If we are to live more sustainably, we need to change our mindsets, because in the end, there is no such thing as waste, only wastefulness.

About the Author

Based in Victoria, Canada, Stephen Salter, P.E. is an engineer with a background in energy and the environment who helps clients reduce pollution, often by reclaiming resources from waste. As a volunteer, he works with local environmental groups to encourage cities to learn from Sweden's practices. His research of Swedish sewage-to-energy schemes was prompted by the city of Victoria's reluctance to upgrade its rudimentary primary treatment of its sewage, which was resulting in dead zones around its outfall pipes.

5. Wastewater at Work

Profiles of Ecological Wastewater Recycling

The following profiles are examples of ecological wastewater recycling at work. They demonstrate a wide range of modalities and approaches based on eco-complexity, featuring rootzone-based treatment, utilization, source separation, and advanced conservation.

SOURCE-SEPARATED SYSTEMS

Waterless Urinal-Graywater System Grows Chicken Feed in Urban Back Yard
Babak Tondre and Rainjita Geesler Residence • Oakland, California

A small fiberglass urinal from Mexico is installed next to the toilet at this urban home. To avoid creating a new plumbing connection for the urinal, it is drained to the overflow drain of the bathtub. All graywater that drains from this tub combines with the urine in an outdoor graywater system consisting of a sequence of three in-ground 50-gallon containers (city trash bins with broken wheels). Each is partially filled with gravel or woodchips. Two cells grow bulrushes and reeds. In the third container, water hyacinth rapidly proliferates in a third container. Tondre adds the water hyacinth to the kitchen scraps he feeds to his chickens, which provide eggs nearly every day. He also irrigates his garden with water from the third treatment cell.

This back yard shows a tight cycle of discharged water and nutrients transformed very locally into high-protein food and points to possibilities for local sustainability and food security. It is also inspiring for its simplicity.

A urinal drains to a graywater system that grows chicken feed and, ultimately, eggs.

Top left: Babak pulls water hyacinth from his graywater-and-urine system and (top right) feeds it to his chickens. And harvests eggs for breakfast (above).

Urine-Diverting Toilets and Composters/Dryers
Gebers • Stockholm, Sweden

Outside of Stockholm, Gebers is a 32-unit eco-logical housing cooperative in a rehabilitated nursing home. Its location next to a lake prompted the residents to use urine-diverting waterless toilets. Urine drains to polypropylene tanks in the basement that are pumped out periodically by a tanker truck and transported to a farm to fertilize animal feed crops. Solids drop to rollaway drying receptacles in the basement. When a receptacle is full, usually every six months, it is disconnected and moved to a finishing area in the corner of the basement. After a year, it is emptied outside and composted further before it is applied to flower gardens. Checking and emptying the receptacles is the responsibility of each condominium owner.

"Ecological living is like composting: What you need is not so much a container as an understanding of a process."
— Robert af Wetterstedt, National Association of Tenants' Savings and Building Societies Environment Section

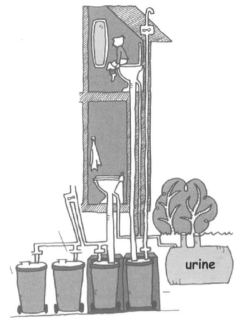

urine

composters

A urine-diverting toilet (left) drains to tanks in the basement (center) that are tested and periodically pumped out for application on grain and hay crops. Solids drop to rollaway composters (right).

Urine-Diverting Flush Toilets in a Designated Nitrogen-Sensitive Zone
Alison Flynn and Seth Wilkinson Residence • Orleans, Massachusetts

All of Cape Cod, a peninsula of Massachusetts, is deemed a nitrogen-sensitive zone where both lakes and seacoasts are overloaded with nutrient runoff from the growing development in this region. Many new buildings are required to reduce nitrogen outputs by half of the volume of a typical development.

The home of Seth Wilkinson and Alison Flynn in Orleans features a a water-flush urine-diverting toilet that flushes urine to a 1,000-gallon outdoor in-ground tank. Feces are flushed to a conventional septic system. The urine tank has a level alarm that signals when it is close to full; however it automatically overflows to the septic system's distribution box.

Inside the toilet bowl, a small partitioned drain in the front of the toilet bowl, so urine is caught and flushed with about one-third cup of water. Solids are flushed with 1.2-gallons of water.

The stored urine-water mixture can be pumped out and used for tree farms or hay crops. The couple plans to install an engineered GROW-N™ (Garden Recycling of Wastewater Nitrogen) planter system with plants specially chosen for their nitrogen- and salt-uptake abilities.

Installing a small garden system to grow away the urine's nitrogen is expected to save significant costs over the expense of buying and operating a powered in-ground denitrification system. In addition, the planted system will double as a landscape and garden feature.

Interior Graywater Systems

The idea of using graywater indoors to irrigate plants is compelling to many who would like to see their flows immediately transformed into delightful plants nearby. But this presents challenges.

Draining a bathtub full of steamy graywater into a planter can add humidity to a building not designed for much interior moisture. Sugars from molds and leaf drop can attract insects. The slightly organic scent of microbial breakdown should be considered before creating interior water-intensive plantscapes.

Controlled air circulation and ventilation, as well as partitioning off interior graywater systems can help to manage these issues.

Sustainable House of Cambridge
Cambridge, Massachusetts

At this four-family house renovated with green building features, graywater is pumped through sand- and gravel-filled planters built into bay window alcoves. They are planted with broad-leafed tropical plants. The local plumbing commission required graywater to first drain to pump basins in the basement. From there it is pumped up to the planters, which overflow to the sewer. In-line Orenco septic tank filters in the pipes filter out particles, Filtrol 160 bag filters fibers from the washing machine. Grease interceptors serve the kitchen sinks. Diverter valves allow redirecting the graywater to the sewer.

Wellfleet Bay Audubon Sanctuary
Wellfleet, Massachusetts

A planter in a hallway at this educational facility managed graywater from public bathrooms. It was first planted with grapevines, but when water pooled in the system, it was emptied of soil and vines and refilled with gravel and broad-leafed tropicals to provide faster evapotranspiration. It overflowed to an outdoor evapotranspiration bed planted as a butterfly-attracting garden. In 2007, the system was replaced with a peat-based wetland when more sinks were installed, increasing the graywater volume.

www.massaudubon.org

Above: A planter in a bay window alcove is irrigated with graywater. Right: A built-in planter in a hallway is part of a graywater system at an Audubon nature center.

Earthships • New Mexico

Created for desert living, Earthships are organically shaped dwellings designed to be as self-sufficient as possible for heating, cooling, electricity, and water. They are constructed of tires packed with earth and encased in a concrete-and-adobe mixture to provide low-cost thermal storage and insulation in the alternately blazing and freezing desert.

Water features include huge water and rain cisterns, experimental solar-heated septic systems, and interior planters that treat graywater for toilet flushing. The planters feature a series of deep and shallow treatment compartments filled with gravel and plants separated by baffles. A mesh bag of wood chips in one compartment serves as a filter. After a few days' retention in the planter, the water is pumped through a carbon filter then used to flush toilets. The sound of the pump accompanies every toilet flush. This close-coupling of use and reuse in the house adds delight and fits the organic forms of these buildings.

Earthship designer Michael Reynolds noticed Earthship residents often neglected to maintain the grease interceptors, so he experiments with using solar heat to dessicate the scum layer from a grease interceptor.

Some Earthships feature septic tanks and leachfields cast into the sides of the buildings.

www.earthships.org

Top: A rainwater-supplied sink and graywater-flushed toilet with an Earthship's treatment planters. Above, a simple do-it-yourself grease interceptor. Left: A graywater treatment planter is part of the kitchen.

Indoor Graywater Planters and Composting Toilets in Office Building
Society for the Protection of New Hampshire Forests • Concord, N.H.

At the LEED-certified headquarters of this forest conservation nonprofit, graywater is filtered and drained to drip-irrigation lines in planter boxes planted with broad-leafed pothos in soil in a central atrium that is also the building's stairwell.

Graywater from the kitchen sink and dishwasher drains to grease-and-sediment traps in the basement. These small tanks with baffles to hold back solids that sink and greases and particles that float, so they can be skimmed off and discarded periodically. After leaving the grease trap, this flow combines with graywater from four bathroom sinks, a utility sink, and a shower and passes through two filter bags made from pantyhose, then seeps through a layer of coal slag (a carbon filter) to a pump chamber. The wastewater passes through a final small-micron filter before being pumped to the second-floor planter boxes.

For blackwater, the facility uses two composting toilet systems, a Clivus Multrum and a Phoenix, with waterless toilets.

About half of the graywater is used by the plants. The rest is drained to a sampling tank then pumped outdoors into drip-irrigation lines in a wildflower bed.

www.spnhf.org

Graywater System Doubles as 19th-Century Garden
The Old Manse, Concord, Massachusetts

The Old Manse is a historic 19th-century house that was once home to American Transcendentalist authors Ralph Waldo Emerson and Nathaniel Hawthorne. Thousands of visitors tour the house annually. It is next to the Minuteman National Park and owned by the Society for the Protection of New England Antiquities (SPNEA).

When the Old Manse's gift shop and offices were expanded, the town required an upgrade to the existing septic system. Due to the site's proximity to the Concord River and SPNEA's plans to conduct an archaeological study of the site, SPNEA required an onsite wastewater system that would not pollute the river or require excavation.

The solution was a blackwater-graywater sep-

arated system. A SeaLand one-pint flush toilet drains to an EcoTech Carousel composting toilet system in the basement. Graywater from the bathroom sink flows to a grease interceptor in the basement then to a pump chamber, in which a float switch turns on a pump when 40 gallons fill the chamber. Liquid from the composting toilet also drains to this pump chamber. From there, this mix is pressure-dosed to a Washwater Garden evapotranspiration planter-bed system consisting of three 18-inch-deep trenches filled with gravel substrate. This system evapotranspires graywater, nutrients, and pathogens.

The Washwater Garden, developed by David Del Porto, was installed on the site of a pre-existing 19th-century theme garden typical of a home of this era. SPNEA planted it with the same varieties used before. Visitors to the house do not know that it is also part of the home's wastewater system.

The extremely low blackwater flow, with solids filtered by the composting toilet system, eliminated the need for a septic tank. Some challenges: The installation in the basement of an air-intake for the house's heating and cooling system drew odor out of the basement and the composter and into the rest of the house. Also, the design was based on a higher graywater flow, so graywater and composter leachate accumulated for overly long periods in the pump chamber before being pumped to the Washwater Garden. The composter's fan occasionally drew odor from the pump chamber. These issues have been remedied but serve as a caution for those who would install water-flush composting toilets with fans.

www.ecological-engineering.com

Composting Toilets and Greenhouse-Enclosed Graywater System
Weiss Residence • Montague, Massachusetts

"Install an ecological wastewater or demolish" was the ultimatum to a property owner by the local health agent. The home had been constructed on a soggy lot surrounded by marsh, crossed by a stream, and adjacent to the next town's water supply wells.

Groundwater levels were too high for a conventional wastewater system, and the proximity to a town's drinking water supply made it too high risk for anything but a zero-discharge wastewater system. Holding tanks are often used in such situations, but health agents know that holding tanks can leak and sometimes develop holes of suspicious nature when property owners face the reality of frequent tank pumpouts at a high per-gallon price.

A zero-discharge strategy starts with conservation. Faucet aerators and a water-conserving washing machine were installed. The water usage by the home was ultimately measured at a mere 11 gallons per day.

An Ekologen WM-ES urine-diverting toilet drains to a four-compartment Carousel composting toilet. Urine diverts to a woodchip-filled compartment within the composting toilet. A small self-contained composting toilet serves an upstairs studio. Graywater from all the fixtures and washing machine drains to a Washwater Garden, a concrete-lined graywater planter bed enclosed by a conventional lean-to greenhouse attached to the house. The greenhouse provides passive solar heating for the house and keeps the graywater system warm and sheltered from precipitation. An outdoor system would require more land area to accommodate rain.

Graywater from the kitchen is first filtered with a grease interceptor underneath the sink. Fibers from the washing machine discharge are filtered by a cloth bag filter.

www.ecological-engineering.com

Left: Ginger, elephant ear, and dwarf bamboos grow away graywater. Above: The exterior of the greenhouse, which serves as a cold-weather living area for the home's owners.

Micro-Flush Toilets, Low-Cost Site-Built Composting Toilet Systems, Rainwater Collection, and Sheltered Washwater Gardens
Lalati Resort • Beqa Island, Fiji

Lalati is an ecologically oriented resort on Fiji's Beqa Island. Lalati's owners wished to protect the nearby coral reef that draws divers from around the world. Even low levels of nitrogen from septic systems can harm coral reefs, so they sought an alternative.

All Lalati's guesthouses feature steeply sloped roofs traditional to Fijian homes for their interior cooling value. Each galvanized aluminum roof has a high lip around the eaves to collect rainwater. Rainwater drains to a large cistern beneath each guesthouse. From there, it is pumped up through a filter and used for all the guesthouse's water uses, from sinks to toilets. Rainwater collected in cisterns was tested for pathogens and found to be well within safe parameters for drinking.

Lalati's owners wished to install composting toilets but shipping costs from North America and Europe were too high, so they had some built. David Del Porto created a portable version that could be used with a flush toilet, a system based on a composting toilet system he designed for Greenpeace in the Pacific islands.

SeaLand micro-flush toilets flush with one pint of rainwater to composters made of 50-gallon (200-liter) rollaway trash bins. Bags made of old fishing nets line the bins so the contents are aerated on all sides. Liquid drains to a Washwater Garden evapotranspiration bed that extends across the rear of each guesthouse. Graywater from a shower and sink also drains to this bed. Each gravel-filled bed is 18 inches deep and planted with local gingers, bird of paradise, and broad-leafed plants native to Fiji. A Lexan translucent plastic overhang extends from the roof to shelter the system from heavy rain that could flood the bed.

The composter is vented with a moisture-resistant fan in a vent stack that terminates above the eaves. When one composter fills, it is disconnected from the toilet pipe and leachate drain line then taken to a composting area to further process.

Then, another bin is put into its place at the guest-house. In this way, the system offers nearly limitless capacity (depending on the number of bins) and makes emptying the composter bins easy. Perhaps most notably, guests usually are unaware that they are using composting toilets.

Washwater Gardens also serve the resort's kitchen and dining area. Early on, the owners learned the value of proper sizing of a kitchen grease interceptor (a box with baffles) when hot greasy water leaving the dishwasher surged past

an undersized interceptor. Grease interceptors should be sized to hold the volume of a sink or dishwasher, so greases can cool and float to the surface for removal. Instead, the greasy liquid covered the gravel and plant roots, requiring the entire garden planter to be dug up and replaced and a new large interceptor installed.

This system is a low-cost and easily replicated and scaled-up zero-discharge ecological wastewater system. With adaptations for flow rate and climate, this system is feasible for a wide range of applications.

www.ecological-engineering.com

Right: A Washwater Garden treats graywater and leachate from a composting toilet (above, shown open) used with a micro-flush toilet (left) flushed by a foot pedal with one pint of rainwater.

Composting Toilets, Rainwater Collection for Sinks, and Parking Lot Bioswale
Chesapeake Bay Foundation's Philip Merrill Environmental Center • Annapolis, Maryland

Three huge wooden water tanks figure prominently at the front of the Chesapeake Bay Foundation (CBF) headquarters located on the shore of the bay. Reclaimed from an old distillery, the tanks were once used to brew beer. Today, they contain several hundred gallons of rainwater collected from the recycled galvanized steel roof and drained through a simple particle filter to remove leaves, etc. before storage. From the tanks, it is filtered with a sand filter and used to supply the building's sink taps, as well as for cleaning, laundry, landscape irrigation, and fire suppression. This water supply eliminated the need to upgrade the site's infrastructure for city-supplied water. Because the rainwater is not disinfected, signs above faucets warn not to drink the water.

Ten waterless toilets drain to three large Clivus Multrum composting toilet systems serve the building's bathrooms. They divert nutrients from the nitrogen-sensitive bay. The contents of the composting toilet systems are managed by the building's facilities manager.

CBF reports the building uses less than 90 per-cent of the water used by a typical office building of its size. The building was one of the first to receive a LEED (Leadership in Energy and Environmental Design) platinum rating, its highest rating.

The Chesapeake Bay is considered a threatened ecosystem, with many species reduced by nitrogen and other pollutants from land activities.

Built in the 1990s on the former site of a beach club, the building features solar hot water heating, under-building parking to minimize its footprint, passive solar heating through south-facing windows, and a geothermal ground-source heating and cooling system. The visitor parking lot is porous paving with stormwater runoff directed to a planted wetland-like bioswale (stormwater retention and infiltration features) to treat oils and tire rubber residue before entering the bay. The surrounding landscape features drought-tolerant native plants to minimize irrigation and mowing.

www.savethebay.cbf.org

Graywater Treatment Pond
Northern California Permaculture Institute • Point Reyes Station, California

Behind a wooden gate at the Northern California Permaculture Institute, a tiny Eden serves as a model of intensive gardening and building with earthen materials.

Gardens are arranged along curving paths that skirt the shade of dwarf fruit trees. Composters, a movable chicken pen, galvanized steel ponds, an outdoor bed enclosure made of bamboo, and a small studio built of clay in the shape of a sleeping dragon (with an abalone shell for an eye and an earthen oven for a mouth) are all tucked onto this one-acre lot. The center's directors live in a small cottage on the site.

A picture-perfect rock-edged pond is home to lotus blossoms, lily pads, and ducks. The three-foot-deep pond is fed by both rainwater from the cottage roof and graywater from its bathroom.

When the pond was first installed, the resident ducks appeared reluctant to enter it. A film of soap and oil seemed to be offputting. To keep the soaps, oils, and carbon from entering the pond, a small subsurface constructed wetland planted with cattails was installed, to the ducks' apparent contentment.

Graywater ponds are not legal in many states, because they potentially expose the public to pathogens. However, treating graywater with a constructed ecosystem before it enters a pond makes this option more acceptable to regulators.

www.regenerativedesign.org

James Stark feeds the ducks in his graywater pond.

Vertical-Flow Graywater Wetland in Cascading Bathtubs
Greywater Guerillas • Oakland, California

In the backyard of a residence in downtown Oakland, water gurgles in two old bathtubs brimming with plants. The home's shower drains into the top tub of this wetland, which is partly filled with gravel and planted with reeds, papyrus, and elephant ear. This tub drains to a lower tub containing no gravel and planted with floating water hyacinth. Its creators, Laura Allen and Cleo Woelfle-Erskine, call themselves The Greywater Guerillas, because they install these systems without legal approvals. Their ideas urban water issues are detailed in their book, *DamNation* (Soft Skull Press, 2007).

They estimate the top wetland retains the graywater for a day and a half before it flows over to the finishing tub pond below. The system's users manually remove graywater from the lower wetland to irrigate the yard's gardens. Drip irrigation line or perforated pipe could be connected to the lower wetland to distribute the graywater.

To keep plant roots and substrate from clogging the drains, they cover them with upside-down plastic milk crates with screen covering it. Unless this system is sheltered, it is advisable to divert graywater to the sewer so the system does not overflow when it rains.

A three-tub graywater system at the Rhizome Collective in Austen, Texas inspired by The Greywater Guerillas. (Photo: Scott Kellogg)

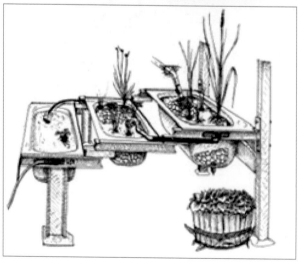

Laura Allen next to her graywater system. Above: A diagram of the system. (Illustration: Annie Danger)

Vacuum-Flush Toilets, Methane Digester to Agricultural Use at Student Residence Hall
Agricultural University of Norway • Aas, Norway

At a residence hall serving 48 students, blackwater and graywater are kept separate for beneficial use.

The bathrooms use 0.26-gallon (1-liter) vacuum-flush toilets that drain blackwater to a tank, from which it is then pumped to an aerated silo composter. Solid carbon waste is added to increase the composting rate, which reaches temperatures of 131° F (55° C). The outputs are a composted solid product and a liquid that is trucked away and used on farm fields as a fertilizer.

Graywater is directed to a septic tank then to a constructed wetland for treatment before discharge to the ground.

By keeping blackwater separate, 90 percent of the nitrogen and 85 percent of the phosphorus in wastewater (when phosphate-free detergent is used for laundry) is diverted, according to the system's designer, Petter Jenssen. His testing shows 97 percent removal of BOD, 99 percent of phosphorus, and 97 percent of nitrogen via the septic tank and constructed wetland.

Jenssen says the vacuum-flush toilets use moderate electricity. The recent development of "vacuum on demand" systems, which provide vacuum power only when needed, use even less electricity. A solar-powered version could use as little as 4 kWh per person annually.

www.umb.no

Vacuum toilet and bidet in student housing. Right: A diagram of the system at Aas. (Photo: Petter Jensen)

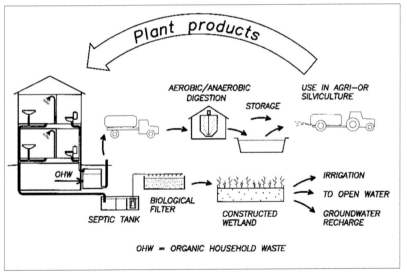

Sink and Washing Machine Graywater Treated in an Evapotranspiration System
Del Porto Residence • Newton, Massachusetts

A graywater system can also manage just one flow. Inside a two-story solar greenhouse built to heat David Del Porto's home outside of Boston, graywater from one of the home's sinks is filtered, treated in aerobic substrate-filled planter beds, then drained to a fountain and pond with resident koi fish and floating water hyacinths.

Outside, what looks like a bed of evergreen shrubs is actually a lined and insulated graywater system irrigated by his filtered laundry machine effluent.

www.ecological-engineering.com

Graywater Treated in Landscape-Integrated Troughs
Naylor Residence • Stevenson, Maryland

Long path-like wooden planks spaced every two feet amid the shrubbery and flowers in Cassandra Naylor's backyard are actually covering five-inch-deep "troughs" to which her graywater discharges. The system, called Nutricyle, was developed by John Hanson for his composting toilet customers. From a surge tank in the basement, graywater flows to the series of troughs, flooding them then seeping through the soil to the rootzones of surrounding plants. Other similar systems by Hansen feature lengths of 12-inch pipe cut in half under which the graywater is discharged.

www.nutricyclesystems.com

Rainwater and Laundry Graywater Irrigate Landscapes at a Public Housing High-Rise
Atherton Gardens • Fitzroy, Melbourne, Australia

Both stormwater and laundry graywater are treated on the landscape of Atherton Gardens, a public housing project comprising four high-rise towers of 760 households.

Rainwater on the roofs is collected and stored in tanks previously used as water tanks for fire suppression. Graywater from the towers' laundry facilities is collected, filtered, and treated via a vertical-flow subsurface wetland that uses recycled glass as substrate. The treatmed graywater is combined with the rainwater and used to irrigate the site's gardens.

According to the Melbourne public housing authority, more than 12,000 indigenous trees, shrubs, groundcovers, and flowering plants are attracting native birds back to the area. Several nesting boxes for bats, parrots, and ringtail possums were installed in existing trees to provide habitat.

Stormwater runoff on the site is captured and treated with bioretention swales and raingardens to keep this flow out of the municipal sewer.

www.ecoeng.com.au

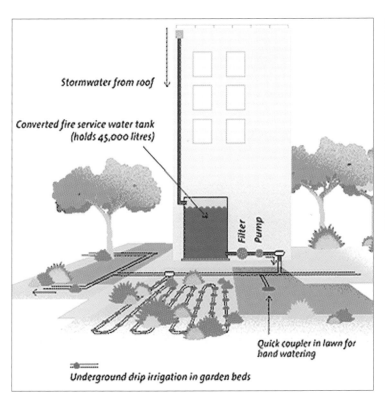

Graywater Diverted to Three Season-Specific Uses
Abasz Residence • Finland, Minnesota

This system on the shore of Lake Superior discharges graywater to one of four destinations: a greenhouse in the spring, an orchard in the summer, the lawn in the fall, and to a 4-foot-deep leachfield-type trench during the winter. The flow is routed by turning a valve that precedes each distribution line. The pump runs twice a day for three minutes at a time to distribute the graywater.

From the house, graywater first flows to a 500-gallon (1,900-liter) Norwesco plastic spherical septic tank (to satisfy regulations requiring a septic tank and also to settle and float particles and soap scum) then a 300-gallon (1,100 liter) tank filled with 3/4-inch gravel and a float switch (in a PVC culvert) that turns on a pump that moves 30 gallons at a time to 1/2-inch perforated pipe inside three-inch drain tile. This thwarts plant root clogging and avoids the need for gravel-filled trenches.

The system's designer, David Abasz, first tried a sand filter to treat the graywater before it discharged to drip lines but found the sand and the drip-irrigation tubes clogged frequently.

www.round-river.com

Graywater Treated in Landscaped Branched-Drain System with Woodchip Basins
Residence • Santa Barbara, California

A home in Santa Barbara, Calif., features a branched drain system that distributes graywater to woodchip- and mulch-filled basins dispersed throughout a landscape. The basins must be replaced every five years to refresh the woodchips and remove nondegradeable fibers. Designed by Art Ludwig, the system works in temperate climates and requires only gardening tasks to maintain it.

www.greywater.net

Photo: Art Ludwig, *Create an Oasis with Grey Water*

Graywater Recycling, Rainwater Use, and Ultra-Conservation at Office Building
The Robert Redford Building • Santa Monica, California

The Natural Resources Defense Council's (NRDC) LEED platinum-rated office building achieves a 50 percent water savings—tens of thousands of gallons per year—compared to similar buildings, according to NRDC.

The building uses filtered and disinfected graywater from showers and sinks, as well as collected rainwater, to supply its nonpotable uses. This reduces the use of potable water for sewage conveyance by 90 percent. Its dual-flush toilets use 0.8 gallons (3 liters) of water to flush urine and 1.6 gallons (6 liters) to flush solids (there is a separate flush button for each). Waterless urinals serve the men's room.

Two custom-built, 40-foot-long rain cisterns, hidden beneath large planters of bamboo, store roughly 3,000 gallons (11,350 liters) of rainwater. This and graywater collected from showers and sinks are treated with an 800-gpd Equaris aerobic treatment and disinfection system, then used to flush toilets and irrigate the landscape.

www.nrdc.org

Above: Graywater treatment tanks. Right: An aerial view of the NRDC building. (Photos: Daniel Hinerfeld/Natural Resources Defense Council)

Sheltered Planted Evapotranspiration System Replaces Leachfield
Sustainable Watersheds • Portland, Ontario, Canada

To address the primary source of nutrient and pathogen pollution in lakes, septic systems, the Centre for Sustainable Watersheds demonstrates a proprietary zero-discharge planted evapotranspiration system that takes the place of a leachfield.

At the Centre's headquarters in Portland, Ontario, a prototype EcocyclET™ installed in 2004 treats all wastewater from the organization's offices and a four-bedroom residence. It eliminated the need to pump out the site's 4,000-gallon holding tank.

Fronted with a septic tank, the system is lined and manages 300 to 475 gallons (1,200 to 1,800 liters) per day.

Wastewater is circulated in a lined shallow bed filled with sand, crushed stone, and gravel with plantings specified for their evapotranspiration abilities in the cold climate of the site. It can be used to manage leachate from septic tanks, composting toilets, or graywater alone.

The system is covered with a carport-type roof made of transparent polycarbonate-panels on the south side to let in sun while keeping out precipita-tion that would necessitate a larger system to manage the extra water.

Installations vary in size as well as landscaping adaptations to terrain and topography. They may be configured in the open, under a roof, or enclosed in a greenhouse.

The EcocylET system is a patented, engineered system developed by David Del Porto of the Ecological Engineering Group based on evapotranspiration research by University of Toronto environmental engineering professor Alfred Bernhart. This system was approved by the local municipal authority and is monitored by the Department of Civil Engineering at Queen's University. In the U.S., it is approved in Massachusetts, Wisconsin, and other states.

The Centre for Sustainable Watersheds sought to protect lake health by promoting a specific nutrient-diverting solution, as opposed to simply educating the public about watershed health problems.

www.watersheds.ca
www.ecological-engineering.com

NEIGHBORHOOD SYSTEMS AND HIGH-RISE BUILDINGS

Greenhouse-Enclosed Sequenced-Aquaculture System Grows Flowers and Flushes Toilets
Julian Woods Community • Julian, Pennsylvania

A Solar Aquatics sequenced aquaculture system manages 1,200 gallons (4,541 liters) of wastewater daily for the 12 homes of Julian Woods, a cooperative community on 140 acres. Community members chose this system over a packaged activated-sludge plant when state regulators required them to upgrade their wastewater systems from the simple composting toilets and pit latrines they were using. The site's clay soil and high groundwater required an advanced treatment system. With help from a state grant, combined with their own funds and labor, community members built the system themselves with hired equipment operators. After 18 months of pilot operation, it was approved as an alternative system. Its engineer estimates it cost 30 percent more than a conventional packaged plant with chemical phosphorus removal and discharge to a stream. Community members decided the cost difference was eliminated by operating the system themselves.

Wastewater enters a 1,000-gallon tank, then flows through 4-inch-diameter pipes by gravity to two septic tanks in series located just before and uphill from the greenhouse. It then flows to a standpipe in the end of a constructed wetland bed, which is 2 to 3 feet deep and filled with 0.75-inch gravel. On the other side of the wetland, two small pumps circulate the effluent back over the top of the marsh, then transfer it to a series of five clear-sided aquaculture tanks constructed of heavy plastic film placed inside steel mesh silo structures. A blower with diffusers bubbles air into each tank. Plants suspended or floating in each tank include watercress, water hyacinth, and papyrus. As the wastewater flows through the tanks via gravity, nitrogen is both removed and a bit is taken up by plants. Julian Woods might alter this so that effluent is first circulated through the aquaculture tanks as in most systems of this type.

The treated effluent then flows through an open sand filter and into a second gravel-bed constructed wetland, which is much like the first wetland, for polishing. On the other side, the effluent is pumped through an ultraviolet disinfection unit

and into a 1,000-gallon (3,800-liter) storage tank. From there, half the flow is pumped to homes to flush toilets and the other half flows to the greenhouse evapotranspiration beds where flowers are grown to sell at a farmers' market.

The evapotranspiration beds are plastic-lined planters containing sand and gravel, with a geotextile (permeable cloth) between them. A drain in the gravel layer connects to several 12-inch diameter standpipes, which provide access to the treated wastewater. Small pumps in some of the standpipes periodically spray the bed surface to help maximize evapotranspiration.

A large exhaust fan and automatic louvers move humid air out of the 6,000-square-foot greenhouse. A small groundsource heat pump heats the greenhouse during the cold months to support biological activity.

The system's engineer says the treatment plant produces produces a high-quality effluent with less than 5 mg/L biochemical oxygen demand (BOD) and suspended solids, less than 0.5 mg/L ammonia, usually less than 10 mg/L nitrate, and less than one fecal coliform per 100 mL. Fecal coliforms before UV disinfection are usually fewer than 20 colonies per 100 mL.

At this point, half the effluent is piped back to houses to flush toilets and a small amount is used to irrigate a cut-flower garden.

Community members received training in wastewater treatment plant operation and now operate the system themselves. The maintenance entails two weekly visits to check components; to record flows, temperature, and water level; and to prune and maintain the plants. Community member Robert Forsberg says it requires no special care, except occasional pump repair and pumpout of the septic tank every three to five years.

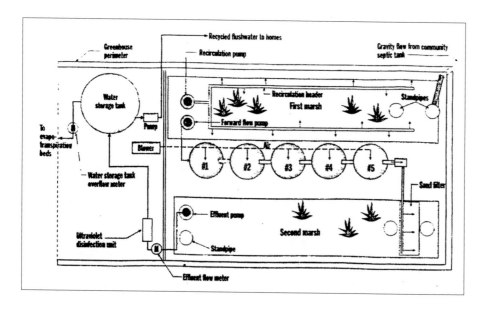

Subsurface-Flow Constructed Wetland for a Village
Jackson Meadow • Marine on St. Croix, Minnesota

Jackson Meadow is a 64-home community designed as a village, with homes clustered together on 40 acres of a 300-acre site located in the historic settlement of Marine on St. Croix.

Clustering the homes preserved 250 acres of open space with six miles of walking trails. Jackson Meadow, with its picket fences and crisp white Scandinavian-style homes, was designed and sited to resemble the town's existing historic farming village built more than 160 years ago.

Instead of installing a conventional leachfield for each home, two constructed wetlands with forced aeration treat a total of 11,000 gallons (3,352 meters) per day from 64 two- and three-bedroom homes. From septic tanks, a lift station periodically doses effluent into a 11,000-square-foot treatment wetland. The treated water is then intermittently injected via a dosing siphon into a 7,600-square-foot (2,200 meters) wetland for pol-

ishing prior to subsurface leachfield distribution.

The wetland is planted to fit into the surrounding restored prairie "to mirror the wetland potholes that once existed across the state," according to its designer, North American Wetland Engineering. Jackson Meadow received state funding to educate and serve as a demonstration of constructed wetland treatment technology.

The forced-bed aeration is used (and patented) by this wetland designer to "overcome the oxygen-transfer limitations of conventional treatment wetlands" and thus boost treatment of nitrogen and other wastewater constituents. This engineering firm, like some others, espouses using aeration and recirculation to optimize wetland performance.

www.jacksonmeadow.com
www.nawe-pa.com

Photo: North American Wetlands Engineering

Subsurface-Flow Constructed Wetland Replaces Failed Leachfield
Grailville • Loveland, Ohio

In 2001, a 1,200-gpd constructed wetland replaced a clogged septic leachfield serving Grailville center's four buildings, including a dining room, laundry, and dormitory.

Four buildings drain to three collection tanks and on to a tank in which a septic tank filter screens 1/16-inch particles. A dosing tank with a high-level alarm pumps at a rate of 200 gallons every four hours. Because wastewater discharge fluctuates widely (the center is full on weekends), a float switch turns off the pumps if the water is too low and signals an alarm if it is too high. A force main pumps water from the dosage tank, under a parking lot, to the wetland. The 50-by-70-foot wetland is 4 feet deep, lined with 45-mil. rubber pond

liner. Substrate is 24 inches of 1-1/2 inch gravel topped with peastone and mulch. Water takes about five days to move through the wetland. Overflow discharges to a leachfield.

The wetland was planted with natives such as river bulrush, dark green bulrush, prairie cord grass, carex comosa, blue flag iris, Joe Pye weed, monkey flower, sneezeweed, and cup plant, which attracts finches. The leachfield was also planted with prairie varieties such as aster, goldenrod, obedient plant, boneset blazingstar, and partridge pea.

Plants are trimmed down in early spring to encourage new growth. The septic filter is hosed down every six months, according to resident Mary Lu Lageman. The center actively promotes this treatment modality to the public and conducts tours regularly.

The site also features stormwater-absorbing raingardens and a butterfly garden.

www.grailville.org

Photo: Grailville

Nutrient-Reducing Rock-Plant Filters to Intercept Leachfield Runoff
Douglas White Architects • St. Thomas, Virgin Islands

As on many islands, septic systems are a hard fit on St. Thomas's rocky ground, with its high water tables and sensitive shoreline always nearby.

After studying the systems of NASA scientist Bill Wolverton, architect Douglas White installed sub-surface-flow rock-plant filters in several of his projects. Designed for intermittent filling, the systems are both aerobic and anaerobic.

For a three-bedroom home's septic tank leachate, he created a 250-square-foot lined 20-inch-deep planter system for a design flow of 330 gallons daily. Tests showed phosphorus levels at 1 and 2 mg/L, nitrogen at zero in the summer and 5 mg/L in colder months, and BOD of 20 mg/L, he reports. White says he chooses local tropical plants for their phosphorus-uptake abilities.

White installs some rock-plant filters downs-lope from leachfields to treat leachate as it migrates down to shorelines. The rock-plant filter also serves as a landscape feature.

Photo: Doug White

All Wastewater Recycled for Toilet Flushing, Landscape Irrigation, and Creating Waterfront Features
Dockside Green • Victoria, Canada

For decades, the greater Victoria region has been infamous for providing only rudimentary screening of its 32 million gallons (120 million liters) of daily wastewater before it is discharged via outfall pipes to the entrance of Victoria Harbour.

By 2006, the city was successfully pressured to implement secondary treatment by citizen and environmental groups such as POOP (People Opposing Outfall Pollution) with its brown velvet-clad mascot, "Mr. Floatie." As of this writing, wastewater treatment modalities are being evaluated.

On a 15-acre former brownfield on the city of Victoria's industrial waterfront, Dockside Green is a mixed business and residential development comprising 26 buildings totaling 1.3 million square feet. It is slated for full completion around 2015.

It is noted for its planned use of many environ-mentally oriented features, such as a waste-wood biomass energy cogeneration system, a mini-transit system, and heating and cooling with alternative fuels.

Particularly notable in light of Victoria's history, Dockside Green plans to recycle much of its wastewater using a membrane bioreactor filtration system that will treat water to potable or near-potable quality. At completion, 702,240 gallons per week—the equivalent of an Olympic-sized pool—will be treated, according to the developer.

The treated water will be used for flushing toilets and irrigating landscaping. What's left will fill a constructed canal-like waterway between two buildings. This creates a waterfront view for the residential units that do not face the sea, and so will increase the market value of these units.

Treated stormwater runoff will also drain to the

A creek that flows between housing units at Dockside Green is fed with recycled wastewater and treated stormwater runoff.
(Photo: Dockside Green)

canal, which will ultimately discharge to the harbor.

The developers estimate that installing water-efficient appliances and recycling wastewater can save 70 million gallons of city-supplied water annually compared to a development without these features. They also estimate that operating costs will be covered by revenues from selling treated water to neighboring buildings. Eliminating the need to upgrade the site's infrastructure for receiving city-supplied water also reduces the capital cost of the system—so much that the development's wastewater treatment will be free, according to the developer.

At the same time, the treated water creates a scenic water feature, an engineered creekside view that realtors covet for its boost to real estate values.

www.docksidegreen.com

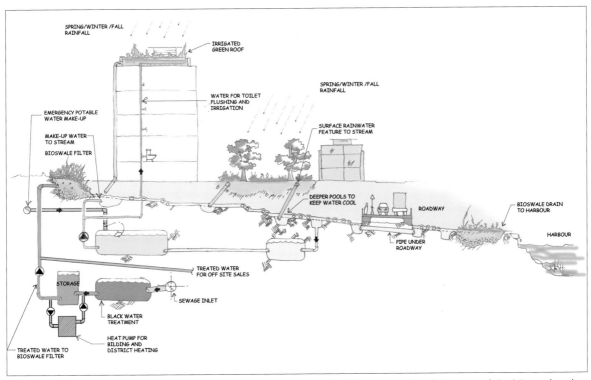

Graphic source: Patrick Lucey and Cori Barraclough

Wastewater Recycling for Flushing Toilets and Irrigation In an Urban High-Rise
The Solaire • Battery Park City, New York City

The Solaire, a 27-story high-rise with 290 luxury rental units in lower Manhattan on the Hudson River, is one of the first green residential high-rises to receive a LEED (Leadership in Energy and Environmental Design) gold rating in the U.S. for features such as high energy efficiency, photovoltaics, a roof garden, and local materials usage.

The Solaire recycles all its wastewater—about 17,000 gpd (64,000 liters)—with a Zenon membrane biological reactor system, with capacity for 8,000 gallons (30,000 liters) more. The treated and disinfected wastewater is used for flushing toilets, cooling tower make-up water, and irrigation of its

park, as well as most nonpotable purposes at its sister building, the Verdesian. In a future building, the recycled wastewater will also be used for laundry machines, according to the developer's water consultant, Ed Clerico. This results in 48 percent less water consumption and 41 percent less waste load to sewers than a conventional building of its size.

Blackwater and sludge residuals from the process are drained to the municipal sewer system. A licensed operator visits the facility twice weekly to maintain it.

Capital cost for the system was $45 per gallon. Clerico estimates it recycles water for about $0.013/gallon, considering all costs. This relatively high cost is due to its small scale. Systems that are five times the size of the Solaire would recycle wastewater for about $0.009 per gallon, he says. As part of an effort to achieve net zero growth in water demand, New York City provides a 25 percent water and wastewater rate reduction for users who install wastewater-recycling systems. This helps offset the costs; however, the reduction applies only to the remaining water and sewer bill, so the more water that is conserved, the less there is left to discount. A better alternative might be an incentive commensurate with the reduction in average water consumption or dual incentives for water demand reduction and wastewater discharge reduction.

Future buildings by the Solaire's developer will use stormwater to augment the recycled water supply.

www.thesolaire.com

Graywater, Rainwater, and Cooling-Tower Condensate Recycled in Office Building
Bank of America Tower at One Bryant Park • New York City

In midtown Manhattan, a 54-story office skyscraper* will supply flush toilets and a cooling tower with rainwater, graywater from lavatory sinks, cooling tower condensate, and some groundwater pumped out of the basement.

Rainwater collected from various parts of the stepped roof drains to cascading steel tanks on floors below, where it is distributed via gravity to flush the building's 250 to 300 flush toilets. All flows, including graywater and cooling-tower condensate, will overflow into a massive storage tank in the base of the building created by waterproofing the cavity inside the core shaft of the building underneath the utility core and elevators. This will provide high-capacity storage for nearly no additional cost. The total water storage is 330,000 gallons (1,248,000 liters). City-supplied water will be automatically added to the tank as a float switch maintains an 18-inch level. The chlorine residual in the city water is expected to be sufficient to prevent biological growth in the tank.

Heating and cooling each draw about 5,000 gallons (18,900

liters) a day. Cooling-tower blowdown and graywater from lavatories will constantly replenish the tank. The system will provide for about half of the building's water needs, about 7.7 million gallons, while diverting 95 percent of the site's stormwater from the city storm sewer.

The combined flows will be filtered by a sand filter, then disinfected with ultraviolet light.

The building uses conserving toilets, waterless urinals, and low-flow fixtures. The plumbing engineer for the project says the dual-plumbing system added significant costs to the project with no short-term payback given the low cost of New York City's water. Unlike in a residential building, a dual-plumbing system in an office building is relatively easy to install, because most lavatories are in the core of the building, and thus in the same place on nearly every floor. Graywater from sinks in the core lavatories will be used, not the potentially higher-strength graywater from the building's various kitchens and private suites.

www.durst.com

*The building was under construction as this book went to press.

VILLAGE AND URBAN SYSTEMS

Polishing Wetland for Municipal Treatment Plant Doubles as Wildlife Sanctuary
Arcata Wastewater Treatment Marsh and Wildlife Sanctuary • Arcata, California

On nearly any given day, joggers, strollers, and birdwatchers roam paths winding through the wetlands of a wildlife sanctuary on the coast of northern California's Humboldt Bay.

Many are unaware the wetlands are polishing wastewater from a treatment plant before it is discharged into the ocean.

In 1977, new regulations restricted the discharge of wastewater into enclosed bays and estuaries. The city of Arcata faced a proposal by the state to build a new plant with a pipeline across the bay to discharge the town's sewage into the ocean.

Instead, some locals proposed an alternative that transformed the existing treatment plant's oxidation ponds into treatment wetlands that would polish wastewater to a quality that could be discharged to the bay.

Today, wastewater from the 2.75 million gpd secondary-treatment plant enters the two oxidation ponds, then passes into a 41-acre intermediate treatment marsh. It is chlorinated and dechlorinated before flowing into a series of constructed wetlands that are also a 31-acre designated wildlife sanctuary. Then it is pumped into the bay.

The intermediate marsh, which is two 45-foot stretches of open water, removes suspended solids from the effluent prior to chlorination and dechlorination. It also provides habitat for fish that eat mosquito larvae.

Creating wildlife habitat provides dual-purpose infrastructure and replaces much-needed displaced habitat. However, as in all free-water or surface wetlands, bird and animal excretions add fecal coliform and nutrients to the effluent, and leaf drop adds BOD. This must be factored into the design.

Common bird species in the wetland include ruddy, teal, and mallard ducks, egrets, herons, sandpipers, ospreys, black-crowned night herons, and marsh hawks. More than 200 resident and seasonal bird species frequent this major stopover on the Pacific Flyway.

The entire sanctuary covers 154 acres, which include "Mount Trashmore," a grassy hill created from a landfill.

Low-Energy Wastewater Treatment Irrigates a Park
Ecoparque • Tijuana, Mexico

In a neighborhood in Tijuana, a city on the United States-Mexico border, a low-energy wastewater treatment and irrigation system was installed in 1986 to show the feasibility of village-operated wastewater systems and the potential of treated wastewater to revegetate neighborhoods.

Today, Ecoparque treats wastewater generated by 10,000 people—about 900,000 gallons a day. Wastewater drains downhill by gravity to the system. It is first screened to filter out larger items, then a finer screen filters out smaller organic particles. Every few hours this second screen is emptied manually into a compost pile. Finished compost is sold to area farmers.

The wastewater continues downhill to pass through a tower in which it trickles through a plastic biofilter maze where it is oxygenated and biologically processed. After that, it flows to a clarifier where sediment sinks to the bottom of the tank. The water is recirculated in the clarifier for three 11-hour cycles. It is then used to irrigate the surrounding hillside, resulting in the growth of flowering bushes, fruit trees, and grass, which can be seen from downtown Tijuana.

Except for one small pump, wastewater moves through the entire process via gravity.

Martin Medina, the system's first operator, says the cost of running treatment plant, park, and environmental education area is $50,000 annually, which includes the salaries of eight people and all operating expenses. The system might be updated in the future to feature a treatment process for the watery clarifier sediment, which is now drained to the city's central treatment plant. Treating this in a lagoon or drying bed is likely to produce odors that would offend the surrounding neighborhoods. A subsurface-flow wetland is a possible solution.

Clockwise from far left: The clarifier; the biological processor; after Ecoparque; and before Ecoparque. (Photos: Martin Medina)

Treated Wastewater Replenishes Wetlands and Recharges Water Supply
East Central Regional Water Reclamation Facility • West Palm Beach, Florida

South Florida, like much of that state, is a fast-growing region in danger of overtaxing its water supply, much of which comes from Lake Okeechobee in the Everglades watershed.

To plan for long-term growth and water demand, the city of West Palm Beach converted its wastewater treatment plant to a 10 million gpd indirect nonpotable reuse system. Tertiary-treated disinfected wastewater is distributed to adjacent 1,500 acres of melaleuca-dominated wetlands. From there, some drains to Lake Okeechobee and some flows along a canal, which also collects rainwater, to two lakes and ultimately to the city's water treatment plant. The city first tested the viability of this concept with a 150,000-gpd test site.

It takes wastewater about two years to cycle through the treatment plant, the wetlands, the water supply, and back to the plant as wastewater.

The plant is complex and advanced, using deep-bed denitrification filters, flocculation with polymers, polishing, and then ultraviolet disinfection, so what leaves the system is nearly potable quality. The test site showed that 6 million gpd applied over 770 acres of wetland resulted only in an eighth-inch water-level rise. Some wastewater is pumped to oxidation ditches where it drains via sheet flow to wellfields for aquifer discharge. This expensive system cost $34.8 million, one third of which was covered by grants.

This indirect nonpotable reuse system reduces the city's draw on Lake Okeechobee (which provides 25 percent of water supply), making 60 to 100 million gpd available for Everglade restoration. It also replenishes the Grassy Waters Preserve, a 20-square-mile wetland area that supplies most of West Palm Beach's drinking water.

Part of the wetland is open to the public and features the Grassy Waters Nature Center and trails and boardwalks throughout the wetland.

www.cityofwpb.com

Photo: Camp Dresser McKee

Solar-Powered Treatment Plant Replaces Ocean Outfall with Constructed Wetland
Calera Creek Wetland Restoration and Water Recycling Plant • Pacifica, California

In the 1990s, the city of Pacifica, population 4.5 million, had five ocean outfalls break up in the rough Pacific Ocean.

After a citizens' group considered alternatives with the city's public works director, a new tertiary treatment plant was constructed in 2000. It discharges to a constructed wetland created in a former rock quarry, thus restoring a historic creek and marsh that existed before mining operations moved it. As a result, populations of birds, snakes, and redlegged frogs have returned to the area. A local birdwatcher identified 150 kinds of birds around the wetland. A trail system runs along the half-mile-long wetland, which streams into the ocean.

Citizen volunteer groups grew 150,000 plants for the wetland, using clippings of native plants from the area and growing them in tree nurseries set up around the city.

The 3.6 million gpd plant uses a sequenced batch reactor (SBR) then sand filters before ultraviolet disinfection. Tanks host an anoxic process that reduces nitrogen to less than 1 mg/L and a daily BOD limit of 3 mg/L. Batching allows the plant to be less sensitive to flows and surges, according to its operator.

Sludge is oxidized into a compost-like product with thermophilic digestion that reaches 160 degrees and can produce a Class A fertilizer the city hopes to sell. Currently, it is used to fertilize oats and for landfill cover. This system was recently optimized to prevent release of odors.

The city plans to use some of its treated wastewater to irrigate area ballfields and a golf course when piping and tanks are installed for this.

The plant has installed an 1,800-panel, 300-kilowatt sun-tracking photovoltaic array on the treatment plant's tanks. It produces 10 to 15 percent of the plant's power, saving an estimated $100,000 a year in electricity costs.

A local entrepreneur is moving to install a biodiesel-production facility next to the plant. The proposed operation would use waste oils and greases pumped from city grease interceptors and convert them to biofuel.

The treatment plant cost $53 million to design and construct.

Red-legged frog

Alternating Constructed Secondary-Treatment Wetlands for a Town Treatment Plant Walnut Cove, North Carolina

In 1994, officials in Walnut Cover, North Carolina, considered building a conventional wastewater treatment plant that would use both mechanical and biological processes to clean wastewater. However, as the original cost estimate of $2 million kept rising, a city commissioner proposed a wetland-based wastewater system as a less expensive alternative to the conventional treatment plant. This was not a well-known option, so residents and engineers were skeptical. But the wastewater wetlands system was eventually built for less than $1 million and began operating in 1996. Its operators say it is less expensive to run than a conventional wastewater treatment plant, partly because it does not require 24-hour oversight as other plants with the same flow volume do.

Consulting designer Bill Wolverton proved the efficiency of wetlands for treating wastewater at NASA (National Aeronautics and Space Administration). As part of its research of closed-loop ecological life-support systems for space communities, NASA studied the cleansing powers of the synergistic reactions between plants and the microbiology in their roots (the rhizosphere). Wolverton decided these processes offered more value for terrestrial pollution prevention and remediation than for future habitats in outer space. His books, *Growing Clean Water* (WES, 2000, out of print) and *How to Grow Clean Air* (Penguin Books, 1999) detail his findings in this field.

After settling, wastewater flows into one oxidation pond, then another, where it is sprayed into the air to provide aerobic conditions. It then flows to an S-shaped open water pond with gates to slow the flow. From there, it is directed by a distribution box to one of two long, curved treatment wetlands planted with cattails, which help denitrify the wastewater. Plant material is screened out, and the wastewater is disinfected with chlorine gas, which is then neutralized with sulfur dioxide gas before it is discharged to a nearby creek. By using two alternating wetlands, cattails can be removed from one wetland while another is in use. This improves nutrient removal and prevents plant-mass clogging of the system. The process takes 60 days to complete the treatment process, and 90 days in the winter. The 25-acre site treats 192,000 gallons (726,000 liters) daily.

www.wolvertonenvironmental.com

Photo: Wolverton Environmental

WASTEWATER TREATMENT FOR AGRICULTURAL USE

A Nine-Town Wastewater Recycling Plant Irrigates Fruit and Vegetables
Monterey County, California

A California-grown strawberry in a fruit salad might well have been irrigated with recycled wastewater.

The many controls required for disinfected recycled wastewater assure this irrigation water source is far more likely to be free of pathogens than the groundwater wells and surface water (from rivers, ponds, etc.) typically used for agriculture.

In the 1990s, the region's multibillion-dollar agricultural economy was endangered due to saltwater contamination of groundwater wells. The constant extraction of groundwater was leading to saltwater intrusion, because the nearby ocean was sucked into the aquifer as the freshwater left it. At the same time, several central California towns were facing growth pressures, prompting a need to expand wastewater treatment facilities.

Nine towns collaborated to create a regional wastewater recycling facility that produces 29.6 million gallons of recycled water per day, which irrigate 12,000 acres (4,800 hectares) of food crops, including artichokes, celery, lettuce, and strawber-

ries. The facility was sited adjacent to farm fields to reduce distribution piping. The $75 million project was completed in 1997 after three years of construction. In the future, the plant might supply recycled water for parks and golf courses.

Monterey County is sensitive to public perception of the quality of its recycled wastewater and goes out of its way to educate the public about the facility and its treatment standards.

A representative of a local farmers' cooperative says growers feel more secure with this water source because it is tested constantly. Workers are more likely to drink out of hoses than they were when the water came from the ground with no filtration or testing. An added benefit is the nitrogen and phosphorus content of the water, which essentially provides a small amount of free fertilizer for these usually unfertilized crops. The soils of many farms in California's Central Valley are high in clay content and low in humus.

Salinity, or salt content, of recycled wastewater is still a concern. Salt comes from both the

city-supplied tapwater (from the ground) and from the diets and cleaning products of the water users. Filtering out all salt would require a cost-prohibitive filtration process.

A nine-town wastewater recycling facility for a widely dispersed service area requires a lot of money and piping, costs that had to be weighed against the loss of agriculture in this region. Usually, the full wastewater recycling option proves too costly when factoring in the cost of transporting recycled wastewater to its point of use. Here, the wastewater plant is adjacent to the farms that use the recycled wastewater.

Wastewater is treated to near-tertiary quality (so some nutrients are still present) and receives advanced filtration and chlorine disinfection. Treated water is filtered through a 6-foot bed of coal, sand, and gravel, the same process used for

drinking water. The recycled water is held temporarily in an 80-acre storage pond before it is distributed to farmlands via an underground pipeline system. During the rainy season, it is discharged two miles into the Monterey Bay. The plant's power needs are supplemented by producing methane with the wastewater.

www.mrwpca.org

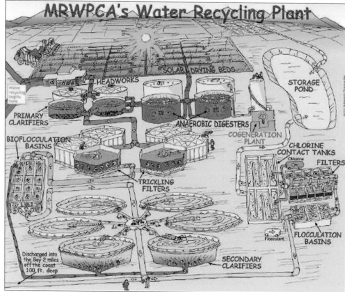

Top: Purple-painted pipes mark the recycled wastewater pumped to irrigate fields.
Above: Tony Valenzuela, director of Quality Assurance and Food Safety for Naturipe Berry Growers, holds a strawberry grown with disinfected recycled wastewater.

Wastewater Biogas Digester Integrated with Agriculture
Biosystem of the Carangola • Petrópolis, Rio de Janeiro, Brazil

A biogas-producing wastewater treatment system for 1,000 people was installed and studied for six years as a training project for engineers of a Brazilian company. The system serves a residential community with a day-care center and a community center.

Sewage, conveyed via a canal covered in floating plants, is first screened by a grate. It then enters a 10-foot-deep (3-meter) sedimentation tank, then flows on to two aeration tanks in which algae starts to form. The sludge is passed to an in-ground methane digester that produces cooking gas for the community center. It flows on to another open tank in which fish, such as pacus, tambaquis, carp, and tilápia, eat the algae and other particles. From there, the water passes to five open tanks of aquatic plants (lemna, pistia, salvinia, azola), which serve as food for fish, ducks, and other animals, and help take up nutrients. The aquatic plants are harvested daily, composted, and used as a soil amendment in an onsite orchard and vegetable gardens. The water is then either discharged to the river or used to irrigate the gardens and orchards.

Ducks are raised as part of the system; they eat plants and insect larvae.

Sludge from the biogas digester and the first screening is removed and dried in the sun for three months, then used as a soil amendment.

A farm research organization analyzed the fertilizer value of the sludge as well as the pathogen content of the food crops grown with the treated wastewater. No helminth eggs, heavy metals, or fecal coliform were present in the composted sludge 54 days after application to the crops nor were they found on birds, volunteers working at the plant, or in the water.

The system is operated by community members, including an operator who lives at the treatment plant and teenagers who apprentice there to learn aquaculture and farming.

www.oia.org.br

Above: A portable cookstove demonstrates the utility of wastewater-produced biogas.

Right: Wastewater circulates through series of open tanks. Plants are skimmed off the top and composted daily.

COMMERCIAL BUILDINGS, NATURE CENTERS, AND PUBLIC FACILITIES

Greenhouse-Enclosed Sequenced-Aquaculture System for a Business District
Weston Center • Weston, Massachusetts

Behind a bank in the center of Weston is a 60-foot greenhouse filled with a jungle of aquatic plants.

In 1995, 10 businesses in the town's center, including a supermarket, were required to upgrade their septic systems and holding tanks. The center is uphill from wetlands buffering the water supply for a nearby city, so advanced treatment was required. The business association chose a Solar Aquatics® System (SAS) sequenced-aquaculture system for its tertiary treatment, attractive appearance, and lack of odor. Although it can treat 10,000 gpd, the SAS was permitted for a maximum of 7,000 gpd due to restrictions on the size of its leachfield. The design is the same as other sequenced-aquaculture systems described in this book, although in this one there is no need for a front-end septic tank to settle and separate the solids. All wastewater drains by gravity to three grinder pumps that chop up the solids and pump the macerated sewage into an aerated blending tank. The blending tank's aeration system both mixes and oxygenates the sewage to homogenize and begin the aerobic microbial treatment. After a few hours in this blending tank, the aerated effluent is pumped to a splitter manifold where it is separated into four equal volumes. The

four volumes enter into four trains of six 5-foot-high clear-sided tanks (solar tanks) planted with floating plants. Air is pumped from the bottom of each tank through diffusers connected to the aeration system. Tiny air bubbles rise up through the wastewater, mixing and aerating it, as well as propelling it to the roots of the plants. After that, the wastewater enters a clarifier where heavier sludge settles, and some clarified effluent is cycled back to the blending tank to reintroduce working microbes to the front end of the system. This activated sludge process is used in traditional aerobic treatment plants to inoculate the incoming sewage with helpful bacteria. The clarified effluent flows into the sand filter and on to a contained constructed anoxic subsurface-flow wetland and UV disinfection before discharge to natural wetlands outside. Variable costs are labor to operate the plant, electricity to run the pumps and air blowers, materials for maintenance and periodic repair, optional heat for the greenhouse, and miscellaneous periodic additives such as sodium bicarbonate and carbon nutrients such as sugars.

Tours of the facility are conducted nearly every week for local school students, university classes, community leaders considering alternative treatment systems, landscape architects, and engineers.

www.solar-aquatics.com

Planted Evapotranspiration System Treats Wastewater for Toilet Flushing and Irrigation
Jordan Lake Business Center • Pittsboro, North Carolina

One of the nicest places to eat lunch at the Jordan Lake Business Center, a former public school converted to an office building, is the arboretum-like courtyard that spans two wings of the building. Enclosed with a translucent roof, it is home to a series of raised-bed planters that double as part of the building's wastewater system, treating about 120 gallons (450 liters) per day.

Wastewater first enters a 2,000-gallon septic tank before draining through an in-line filter to a 1,500-gallon storage tank from which it is pumped through a series of distribution lines into two 2-foot-deep constructed wetland cells.

The first treatment phase is a sequence of three sand filters that drain horizontally into subsurface wetlands at six- to eight-hour intervals. The second cell fills with water and drains, controlled by a solar-powered valve, so it is intermittently aerobic and anaerobic to further denitrify. The water draining from this cell is divided into adjustable proportions controlled with a splitter valve. Some wastewater moves to an ultraviolet disinfection unit from which it is pumped to the courtyard. The remainder can be pumped back to the septic tank.

The disinfected water is distributed to a variety of planters filled with 12 inches (0.3 meters) of sand, with gravel around the distribution pipe, to further reduce suspended solids and nutrients. Plant varieties include liriope grass, wax myrtles, and inkberry.

Solar photovoltaic-powered pumps move the wastewater only during daylight hours, when oxygen levels are highest—thanks to plant photosynthesis. Once through the system (a seven- to 10-day cycle), the treated wastewater flows to a tank that supplies water for toilets and for irrigation of the exterior landscape.

The system's designer, Hal House, chose crushed brick for the substrate, because it is a low-cost recycled waste product and because its iron content helps hold phosphorus and salts. A layer of charcoal was placed just below the surface of the planters to prevent odors from entering the courtyard, he says.

www.waterrecycling.com

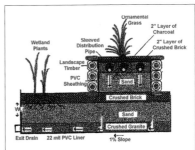

Planter cross-section

Stormwater Wetland Collects Water for Toilet Flushing
The Stata Center, Massachusetts Institute of Technology • Cambridge, Massachusetts

The Stata Center is a signature building on the Massachusetts Institute of Technology (MIT) campus. Designed by postmodernist architect Frank Gehry, it features the surprising angles and titanium surfaces typical of Gehry's work. Providing an organic counterpoint to the building's hard lines, a deep wetland extends across the rear of the building like a moat. (Students call it "the alligator pit.") An elevated walkway over the wetland leads to an entrance. This wetland treats stormwater runoff from the site and recycles it to flush toilets, allowing MIT to divert a significant portion of its site runoff away from the stormwater sewer, as mandated by the city.

Rainwater drains from the roof of the building and some surrounding buildings, entering the wetland from high-level and low-level drains.

High-level drains discharge into the upper portion of the wetland. When full, a level switch starts pumping rainwater to the lower portion of the system. This is an underground rainwater storage chamber made of RainStore units, which are recycled plastic lattice cages that provide storage with internal structure.

The full capacity of the system is sized to manage a 100-year rain event or about 50,000 gallons (189,000 liters). About 2.5 feet (0.76 m) depth of stormwater is maintained in the storage tanks for toilet flushing and wetland flow.

The wetland area in the upper part of the wetland is constantly circulating water. During dry spells, the water in the lower wetland recirculates into the wetland via a solar pump. Stormwater is pumped out of the lower RainStore system and

Photo: Nitsch Engineering

saturates the wetland substrate at a low flow rate (1 gpm). This recirculation provides an opportunity for active microbial and biochemical polishing of any particles or nutrients in the stormwater. Total suspended solids are reduced by 80 percent. The pump is solar-powered by photovoltaic panels on the roof. The toilet-flushing water system consists of 3,000-gallon fiberglass-reinforced plastic water storage tanks, a filtering system, and distribution pumps. A rainwater storage tank is situated between the city water supply and the building's distribution pumps. All pipes are painted the distinctive purple color that signifies nonpotable

water, and purple signage is used on fixtures. A separate city water supply line supplies sinks, showers, and drinking fountains. The city water make-up line to this storage tank has a backflow preventer (a check valve) to protect the building's drinking water system from the nonpotable water in the tank. The collected rainwater flushes both toilets and urinals.

The rainwater is filtered with a sand-and-anthracite multimedia filter to remove particles, then it is disinfected with ultraviolet light to destroy pathogenic bacteria washed from the roofs before the rainwater mixes in the tank with city-supplied water. Because the rainwater storage tank has removed all city water pressure, booster pumps distribute water to the toilets and urinals, particularly in the high-rise building.

One consultant for this project estimates the savings from avoided cost of city-supplied water will cover the cost of the rainwater collection and wetland in three years.

www.bioengineeringgroup.com
www.jnei.com

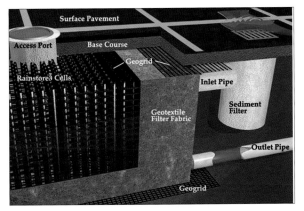

Sequenced-Aquaculture System Recycles for Toilet Flushing, Serves as Science Lab
Adam Joseph Lewis Center, Oberlin College • Oberlin, Ohio

The Adam Joseph Lewis Center, which houses Oberlin College's science classes, was designed as a living laboratory and a model of an ecologically oriented building, with passive solar heating, photovoltaic-generated electricity, low-energy materials, and superinsulation.

Its wastewater is managed by a Living Machine®, a sequenced-aquaculture system that treats wastewater from toilets and sinks. The maintenance and monitoring of the system is incorporated into environmental studies curricula. A Web site for the system shows real-time levels of water, dissolved oxygen, and water usage, as well as views of the system and student research projects using the system.

To educate the rest of the school about the system, the Center has conducted "Poop Campaigns," offering treats to students to encourage them to go to the Center and use the toilets.

Wastewater (mostly from bathrooms) drains by gravity to two 1,500-gallon settling tanks (anaerobic) and on to two 1,500-gallon aerated closed aerobic tanks to nitrify. It then enters a greenhouse-enclosed treatment train of three large above-ground aerated aquaculture tanks in which plants are suspended. It moves on to a 700-gallon clarifier, then to a 4,500-gallon (17,000-liter), 3-foot-deep constructed wetland planted with woolly sedge, willow, iris, and bulrush. It

drains to an ultraviolet disinfection unit and to a 2,500-gallon (9,460 liter) holding tank from which wastewater is pumped to a pressurized holding tank to be ready for use for toilet flushing and irrigation. The school reports tested treated wastewater had a BOD content below 5 mg/L, nitrate at 7.03 mg/L, and phosphate at 2.49 mg/L.

www.livingmachines.com
www.oberlin.edu

Top: The wastewater system of the Adam Joseph Lewis Center at Oberlin College is integrated into the interior of the building. Right: A student washes off a wastewater treatment "plant." (Photos: Oberlin College)

Sequenced Wetlands and Hydroponics to Recycle Wastewater and Stormwater at Spa El Monte Sagrado • Taos, New Mexico

An ecological wastewater and stormwater treatment system disguised as a tropical jungle is integrated into the guest facilities at El Monte Sagrado, an upscale spa in arid Taos.

Next to a swimming pool and hot tub are the treatment tanks, wetlands, and a display pond in which the final effluent flows over a waterfall and into a pond of tropical fish.

All wastewater from the resort's toilets, showers, hot tubs, restaurant, and laundry facilities flows to in-ground settling tanks. From there, the water is pumped through a series of aerated tanks integrated with planters in the greenhouse, called

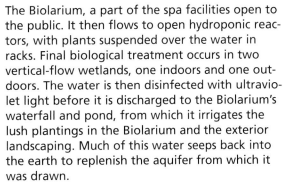

The Biolarium, a part of the spa facilities open to the public. It then flows to open hydroponic reactors, with plants suspended over the water in racks. Final biological treatment occurs in two vertical-flow wetlands, one indoors and one outdoors. The water is then disinfected with ultraviolet light before it is discharged to the Biolarium's waterfall and pond, from which it irrigates the lush plantings in the Biolarium and the exterior landscaping. Much of this water seeps back into the earth to replenish the aquifer from which it was drawn.

Biological oxygen demand (BOD) and total suspended solids are reduced to less than 5 mg/L, and total nitrogen to less than 10 mg/L.

Nearly all the site rainwater and stormwater runoff is collected through an extensive system of roof gutters, drop inlets, and underground drainage pipes and onto a lift station. From there it is pumped into 20,000-gallon storage tanks from which it is circulated through an aerated wetland system.

The treated water also helps flush an outdoor cascading pond system. This water flushed from the ponds is filtered and used to irrigate a lawn.

The system's engineer says it is automated by computer control. Operational checks and routine maintenance require about an hour per week.

www.livingmachines.com

Sequenced-Aquaculture System Serves Highway Rest Area
Interstate 89 Rest Area • Sharon, Vermont

Visitation to a Vietnam War memorial fell off when the state closed the highway rest area where it was located. (The highway reportedly had symbolic significance because it was used by Americans who fled to Canada to avoid the draft during the Vietnam War era.)

To respond to war veterans' concerns about the neglected memorial and to provide nonpolluting wastewater treatment at the site, the state installed a Living Machine system.

In a circular atrium, wastewater flows through a series of concrete tanks in which Southeast Asian plant varieties are suspended. They can be viewed from a deck that is open to the public. (Living Machines, designer of the system, no longer emphasizes this open-tank system design.) The greenhouse is heated and cooled by 24 geothermal wells. A similar system circulates warmth under the sidewalks to melt snow in the winter.

The wastewater treatment system is open to the public and attracts many visitors, who pass the veterans' memorial at the entrance.

www.livingmachines.com

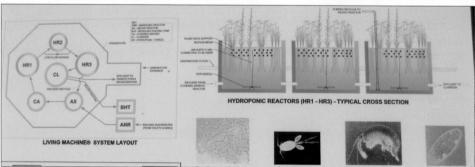

A sign describes how the waste-water system works.
(Photos: Dave Alexander)

Packaged-Treatment Plant Remade as an Aerobic Hydroponic System
Smuggler's Notch Resort • Vermont

When more wastewater treatment was needed at a central Vermont ski resort, it reactivated its old activated-sludge packaged-treatment plant to supplement the existing lagoon system. The 1960s-era treatment plant was converted to a 40,000-gpd hydroponic system by adding plants to the first aerobic tanks. From the aerobic tanks, wastewater flows to anaerobic and anoxic tanks before it is discharged to one of two lagoons. Disinfected wastewater from the lagoons is applied via spray irrigation to nearby forest.

www.livingmachines.com

Sequenced-Aquaculture System Recycles Domestic and Animal Washdown Wastewater
Noorder Zoo • Emmen, Netherlands

The Noorder Zoo receives 1,500,000 visitors annually. A Living Machine sequenced-aquaculture and wetland system at the zoo treats 220,000 gallons (832,000 liters) daily of wastewater generated by both visitors and washing the zoo's animals. Treated wastewater is used onsite to flush toilets and for other nonpotable uses, such as washing animal housing and filling ponds in the zoo's recreated habitats. The zoo claims the system has reduced its water consumption by 84 percent. Wastewater passes by gravity to sequenced wetlands in concrete tanks in concentric circles integrated into the visitor facilities. The plant roots and substrate provide surfaces for bacteria to attach and consume the constituents of the wastewater.

www.noorderdierenpark.nl

INDUSTRIAL AND SUPPLEMENTAL SYSTEMS

Sequenced-Aquaculture System for Biotech Laboratory and Office Building
New England Biolabs • Ipswich, Massachusetts

When this manufacturer of biological DNA testing materials converted a former Catholic school campus into its corporate headquarters, the town required it to install its own wastewater system due to possible unknown biologicals in the company's discharges. This Solar Aquatics System design is the same as the previously described Weston facility but has an actual daily flow of 9,000 to 12,000 gpd (34,059 to 45,000 lpd), about half its permitted discharge flow. This is due to advanced water conservation measures in the buildings. The system uses six treatment trains of four solar tanks, each holding about 1,150 gallons for a detention equal to 27,600 gallons. Typically, the total detention time, including the anoxic subsurface-flow wetland, is 1.5 days from entry into the blending tank to the discharge of disinfected tertiary treated effluent into the final holding tank. From there, two pumps move it to leachfields for dispersal.

To reduce projected costs of heating the greenhouse to support the tropical plants often placed in these systems, the designer specified a native plant palette that would tolerate cooler temperatures. However, the client preferred a tropical planting program, with palm trees and fruit-producing banana trees.

www.solar-aquatics.com
www.ecological-engineering.com

Constructed Wetland Treats Oil- and BTEX-Contaminated Groundwater
British Petroleum • Casper, Wyoming

A huge circular wetland system treats up to 3 million gallons of contaminated groundwater that was the result of 50 years of petroleum refinery operations by Amoco on a site in Casper. The site's current owner, British Petroleum, closed the refinery and worked with the municipality to convert the site into an office park and 18-hole golf course while remediating the accumulation of hydrocarbons, oil, BTEX (benzene, toluene, ethylbenzene, and xylene), and MTBE (methyl tertiary-butyl ether) compounds under the site.

The treatment system is flexible enough to handle 500 to 2,200 gallons (1,900 to 8,300 liters) of water per minute while staying within discharge limits. A pilot wetland was established first to measure performance.

Oil and groundwater are recovered and separated by a system of wells and an enclosed, indoor oil-water separator. Recovered oil goes to storage tanks for recycling. The resulting effluent flows to a cascade aerator that helps reduce the high iron levels that could clog the wetland. It also treats the effluent by helping to gas off the unwanted constituents. The effluent then flows to the surface-flow wetland where the iron is allowed to settle for future recovery, then on to two constructed subsurface-flow wetlands for final treatment. The wetlands are filled with 4 feet (1.2 meters) of crushed concrete (recycled from the site), covered in compost, and planted with native grass species. The radial-flow wetland is aerated from the bottom for accelerated treatment and insulated for year-round operation at temperatures as low as -35°F.

The treated water is then conveyed by a lift station to a nearby lake or the city wastewater treatment plant, or it is re-injected to recover more hydrocarbons.

Installing a treatment wetland saved BP $12.5 million over the cost of conventional mechanical plant treatment, according to the designer.

www.bp.com
www.nawe-pa.com

Photo: BP

Constructed Wetland Treats Winery Washdown Water to Irrigate Vineyard
Benziger Family Winery • Glen Ellen, California

Making wine requires washing down equipment and floors, resulting in an acidic and sugary effluent. At Benziger Family Winery, a 29-by-120-foot (8.8-by-36 meter) constructed wetland treats about 5,000 gallons (18,900 liters) per day of this washdown water, before it is discharged to an irrigation pond from which it is pumped to an irrigation filter and on to drip-irrigation lines throughout the vineyard.

The wetland is three feet deep, filled with peastone, and planted with both local and tropical macrophytes, including gingers and elephant ear. It is preceded by a facultative pond, the surface of which is covered with floating water fern (*Azolla caroliniana* and *Salvinia rotundifolia*) that discourages algae clogging by shading the pond (reducing photosynthesis). It also fixes nitrogen to improve the carbon-nitrogen ratio of the nitrogen-poor wastewater for faster microbial transformation.

System engineer Heather Shepherd of Sebastopol, California, designed this and several other constructed wetlands for vineyards. She also designs graywater systems notable for their use of moisture sensors that divert graywater from the sewer only when the landscape needs it.

Benziger is a Sonoma Valley vineyard that uses both organic and biodynamic practices to grow its grapes; it strives to be a model of responsible low-impact growing. The vineyard provides extensive explanations of grape varieties and their flavors to the public and features an "insectory" that grows plant varieties to attract the birds and insects that are known predators of pests common to vineyards.

www.benziger.com

OTHER SYSTEMS

Floating Aerated Suspended Rootzone System Cleans a Sewage Canal
Baima Canal Restorer • Fuzhou, China

A floating walkway lined with plants helps treat an overloaded sewage canal in the city of Fuzhou, population 6 million.

The "Canal Restorer," a 1,640-foot (500-meter) floating platform with a walkway supporting 12,000 plants of 20 native species, treats the canal water to secondary treatment standards.

The plants are suspended over the water on each side of the walkway in a loose-weave geotextile attached to floats outrigger-style. On the floor of the canal, flat flexible-membrane diffusers, powered with an electrical blower, follow the length of the floating platform. They aerate and move effluent up to the plant roots. This is similar to the process at work in the large aquaculture tanks in the Solar Aquatics, Living Machines, and EcoMachine systems.

Before.

The 2,000-foot (600-meter) canal was polluted by the discharges of an estimated 750,000 gpd of untreated domestic wastewater, causing odors and floating solids. Instead of piping the wastewater sources to a remote wastewater treatment plant, the city sought a treatment system within the canal itself.

The Canal Restorer reduced odors, eliminated floating solids, drastically improved the aesthetics of the neighborhood and the clarity of the water, and reduced the negative impact on downstream aquatic ecosystems. The designer has also applied this system to a eutrophied lake and an animal feedlot manure management lagoon.

www.toddecological.com
www.oceanarks.org

After. (Photos: Todd Ecological)

Rootzone-Filtered Swimming Pool with Rainwater Storage
Private residence • Berlin, Germany

A swimming pool in a southwest district of Berlin integrates plants and ecosystem features to stay clear and acceptably clean for swimmers.

Water naturally circulates through a wetland around the perimeter of the 14-by-6 foot (4.30 m-by-1.8 m) pool, keeping it oxygenated and clear. It is replenished with rainwater collected in two small ponds with streams that trickle to the pool.

The 6.5-foot-deep square pool was formed in loamy and clay soil and was lined with a polyethylene liner. Its lined walls end about 12 inches below the water line, allowing water to move through the surrounding wetlands and small ponds—called purification zones—planted with about 50 species of water-loving plants such as water lilies and iris. The substrate is composed of layers of gravel and sand separated by a geotextile. Water trickles via a cascading rock creek to a lower pond, which features one deep spot for additional treatment.

The pool also serves as rainwater storage. Rain drains from roof runoff pipes to a creek to the pool. Water moves via gravity, but solar pumps could be used.

The pool was inoculated with water from a healthy, oligotrophic lake to help establish a microbiological community.

In combination with a rainwater-harvesting systems, this can be a cost-effective and attractive alternative to conventional chlorine-disinfected swimming pools. Maintenance is the same as that of a garden, including removing biomass in the autumn every year. Sediment buildup on the pool's floor might require mud-pumping periodically.

The plants help oxygenate the water and raise the pH of the slightly acidic rain by precipitating calcium ions on their leaves, according to the designer, Grit Bürgow of Aquatectura Studio for Regenerative Landscapes. The pool has not been tested for bacteria counts or nitrogen, because the risk is low and the pool is for the homeowners' personal use.

www.aquatectura.de
www.ecological-engineering.com

Top: Grit Bürgow inoculates the pool with pond water. Above: The naturally cleaned pool.
Photos: Gruenwerk Landscape Consulting

WASTEWATER SYSTEMS AS ART
Cascading Wetland-Planter River-Cleaning Sculpture
Elevated Wetlands • Taylor Creek Park, Toronto, Canada

The Elevated Wetlands are six giant plastic planters—with legs—helping to clean the Don River in Toronto. A solar-powered pump moves water from riverside ponds to the tops of three planters, where it filters down through a substrate of shredded tires, recycled resin pellets, automobile shredder residue, and plastic bottles, all of which presumably host biofilms just as gravel and other more common mineral substrates do. The water then cascades into the other planters, before spilling into a pond that trickles to the river.

Commissioned by the Canadian Plastics Industry Association "to create a public work of art that brings together both the plastics and art communities," the Elevated Wetlands were designed by

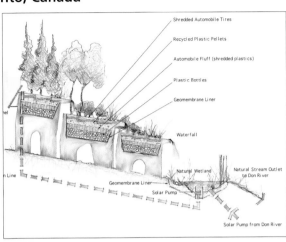

environmental designer Noel Harding.

The animal-like planters were originally planted with local native varieties but plant varieties surrounding the planters ultimately took over, Harding says.

Testing of the water discharged by the final planter showed improved clarity and some reduction of nitrogen.

www.elevatedwetlands.ca
www.noelharding.ca

Wastewater-Treatment Sculptures
Jackie Brookner

Jackie Brookner's artwork explores origins and interfaces of human and plant life in nature's cycles.

Her sculpture *Prima Lingua* ("first language" in Latin) is a massive 5-foot-high ceramic tongue on which mosses and ferns grow. The piece is in a basin filled with volcanic rock and macrophyte plant varieties, such as taro and papyrus. Water originally collected from farm runoff is circulated up and over the tongue, where microbial life in the plant roots and pores in the tongue's surface filter and stabilize the runoff's nutrients as it trickles back into the pool. Brookner calculated the piece can clean 70,000 cubic feet of air in a room in one week. Snails, salamanders, and other creatures in the pool add to the diversity of the system.

Brookner's other work includes landscape-based pieces with sculptures and plantings that interpret the history of sites. For the office of a nonprofit organization, Brookner created a naturalistic assemblage that treats graywater from a sink at the offices of a nonprofit organization. Water drained from the sink is pumped up and over a

Brookner's water-cleaning sculpture, *Prima Lingua*

Top: A tower of plants cleans graywater from an office sink. Above: A grease interceptor and pump chamber precedes Brookner's graywater-treatment sculpture. (Photos: Jackie Brookner)

five-foot-high assemblage of rocks planted with broad-leafed plants and mosses.

The sculpture, *Gift of Water*, is a naturally filtered swimming pool in Germany featuring treatment wetlands. The water is discharged from the wetlands through a concrete sculpture of moss-covered cupped hands and into a swimming pond. *I'm You* is a moss-covered lava rock on a metal form in the shape of hands. This is suspended above a wetland pond basin filled with reeds and water hyacinth. The lattice-like design of the hands is based on the microscopic structure of mosses. A mister periodically sprays the pond's polluted water onto the hands, which drip it back into the pond.

These systems can also be integrated into malls, botanical gardens, aquaria, cooling shelters, and even wall-mounted living art.

www.jackiebrookner.net

Gift of Water (top and above) is a swimming basin cleaned with wetlands and aerated with a fountain.

Clockwise from top left: Elva Del Porto installs a wastewater treatment "plant," a constructed ecosystem to manage leachate from a composting toilet on an island in Maine; a planted wall is irrigated with graywater; a frog in a constructed wetland serving a lakeside house on Cape Cod; a RainWall stores rainwater and graywater while serving as a small-footprint privacy wall; Carol Steinfeld picks cherry tomatoes irrigated with graywater and urine in front of her office; a floating wetland, held afloat with used water bottles, helps clean a pond.

6. A Resource-Recycling Future

Visions for the EcoWater Frontier
A Prescription for Security, Abundance, and a Return to Earth's Intrinsic Wastewater Treatment "Plants"

In his book *Infrastructures*, Malcolm Wells, architect of landscape-integrated buildings, paints a picture of a future in which our infrastructure doubles as landscapes.

That future is here: Wastewater treatment systems increasingly are tree plantations, gardens, biofuel farms, fields of grain, and forests—the original wastewater treatment "plants" for this planet.

Ian McHarg in his seminal book *Design with Nature*, urged designers and land planners to heed the "intrinsic suitabilities" of sites. Indeed, more and more site planners and architects are viewing cities as whole ecological watersheds with a wide spectrum of flows, hydrologies, and opportunities to clean wastewater at discharge and collection points. Onsite treatment modalities obviate the extensive networks of pipes and pumps that create concentrations of water, nutrients, and pathogens that require lots of energy to treat and dispose of.

Wastewater treatment is turning up in new places: Greenwalls evapotranspire water (and can store it) while providing vertical greenery that cleans air and buffers extremes of temperature and wind. Green eco-roofs, mostly used to reduce stormwater runoff, also treat wastewater, keep buildings cooler during hot months, and provide habitat for birds, bees, butterflies, and building users. Water storage increasingly will be integrated into unused spaces throughout cities.

The roof of the John Deere tractor plant in Germany features a constructed wetland that treats discharges from manufacturing operations. (Photo: John Deere, Inc.)

The water, nutrients, organics, heat, and potential energy in wastewater will become so valuable we might see the term "wastewater" displaced with terms that describe the possible uses of different types of effluents, because the components of wastewater will be in demand to nourish the ecosystem and to provide other beneficial uses. This is the best way to prevent pollution: by not creating it in the first place.

Wastewater management will become a specialty of ecologists, landscape designers, and agronomists, as utilization replaces disposal. As our population grows, we are learning that what we discard comes back to us in various welcome and unwelcome forms. Today, we know how to make less wastewater and how to transform the wastewater we have into food, fuel, and fiber, not unwanted pollutants.

Wastewater likely will become a commodity marketed to biofuel farmers and managers of brownfields, golf courses, cemeteries, highway medians, and other landscapes that need lots of water and nutrients. Economists will find that using wastewater ecologically addresses simultaneously issues of foreign oil dependence, climate change, rising treatment costs, and water pollution.

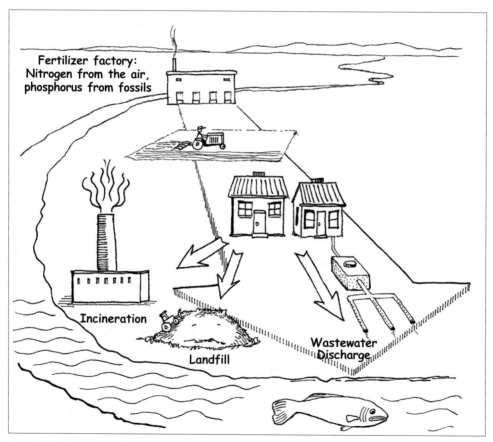

The Nutrient Cycle Interrupted: Nutrients are pulled from air or ground and do not recycle. (Illustration: Dan Harper)

The solutions are here; we have the information we need. Most of the research is done. We don't need to wait for revolutionary new technologies nor for institutions to issue feasibility studies. The age of exhaustively studying possibilities has passed; the challenges—and the opportunities—of our day call us to act now.

Ecological wastewater recycling solutions will provide greener, more delightful and heathful living spaces and communities, with lower energy and operating costs for high performance. As the pricing of water and fuel increasingly reflects their true costs, wastewater innovations currently used solely in response to drought or for green building certification points will become mainstream. The economics favoring utilization over disposal will be more compelling.

And whether it's for love or money or legality, more communities, builders, and property owners will heed the charge of the 21st century to "grow with the flow."

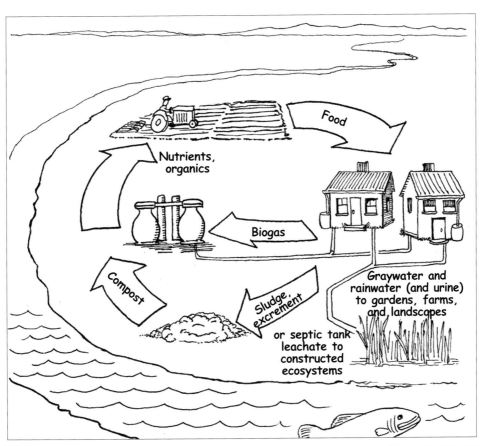

The Nutrient Cycle Restored: Nutrients, organics, and water are used productively. (Illustration: Dan Harper)

Appendix

Commercial Graywater • Graywater Constituents • Wastewater-Reuse Parameters

Using Graywater from Commercial Buildings

Graywater from commercial buildings varies widely depending on what the water was used for. That means there are no sweeping generalizations about how to treat it.

Regulators consider commercial and industrial graywater to be the same as combined wastewater. Although not often stated in the government literature, wastewater is any potable water used for any process after it has departed the faucet, hose bib, showerhead, or plumbing connection and to a water-using fixture or appliance such as a dish or clothes washing machine. In some jurisdictions, only residential wash water is technically graywater. Commercial and industrial washwater is simply wastewater and must be treated as such. However, for the purpose of avoiding confusion here, we will call this effluent "graywater."

Graywater, like wastewater, can be ranked by ease of treating prior to reuse, so you might say there are shades of gray. In wastewater terminology, it is the characterization of the untreated or raw effluent by strength (concentration), constituents (pollutants such as solids, chemicals, pathogens, and nutrients), and volume. The following is a list of graywater sources ranked from the easiest to the most difficult to treat.

1. Clean water is potable water collected in a clean container not mixed with or contaminated by any other substance. An example is a bucket of water transported to a cooking or rinsing site. It has not been "used" in the traditional sense, but it has been placed in a container with dubious sanitation and could pose a health risk.

2. Condensate is water that has been condensed from water vapor. Sources of water vapor include steam from boilers, steam tables, and humid air. In the process of condensing, the condensate can be contaminated by leakage from turbine gland seals, open collection trays and channels, airborne contaminants (in dust or droplets), or from lubricants and other chemicals associated with heat exchangers, other process equipment, engines, electric motors, etc. Care must be taken to remove condensate quickly before contamination occurs. Supermarkets use vacuum systems to collect and remove condensate from refrigerated and frozen food cases. This condensate can be a significant source of water supply not accounted for in the water bill. For example, a medium-sized supermarket's air conditioners and coolers in Massachusetts generated 3,000 gallons of condensate per day during a humid hot summer.

3. Rinse water is what is discharged after washing using soap or detergent to clean cooking utensils, dishes, and laundry. This graywater is of a relatively high quality and low strength as most of the contaminants and detergents have been drained away in the washing cycle. A sand-and-anthracite filter (with optional automatic backwasher) might be sufficient for treating this graywater before irrigation or disinfection.

4. Washwater results from the wash cycle of dish and laundry machines, floor and counter scrubbing, and window washing. It is the most difficult graywater to treat as it contains most of the water volume, chemicals, and pollutants. In restaurants and other commercial food service facilities, it also contains large quantities of troublesome disinfectants, grease, and oil. Effluent from laundry-washing machines has a high concentration of nonbiodegradable lint. During the agitation cycles, textile fibers break off and must be removed to avoid clogging irrigated soils and leachfields. The threads used to make microfiber fleece clothing—nonbiodegradable microfibers, some as small as 40 microns—are clogging soils and leachfields.

5. **Food washwater and washwater** from restaurants and other commercial food service facilities requires pretreatment to reduce greases, carbon, and nitrogen. High surge volumes during busy periods and higher temperatures makes this tricky, because high levels of fats, oil, and grease (FOGs) produce a high biochemical oxygen demand (BOD). FOGs are emulsified and liquefied by high-temperature water and by powerful detergents. When cooled in pipes, reuse equipment, soils, and collecting tanks, FOGs re-solidify. Emulsification of the FOGs suspends them during transport, but they accumulate downstream and cause problems.

6. **Vehicle-maintenance and washing facilities:** While not typically characterized as graywater, washwater from these facilities can be recycled. Today, most car and truck washing businesses treat and recycle the water to save both the water and sewage charges, but the warmth in the water as well. However, toxic chemicals, polyaromatic and polycyclic hydrocarbons, oils, and grease from vehicles require special treatment.

Oil In Water

Oil in water can be present in four basic forms:

1. **Dissolved oil:** Degreasing chemicals and chlorinated detergents can dissolve oil so much it is no longer identifiable as droplets of any size, hence it cannot be removed mechanically.

2. **Free oil:** The majority of oil and grease in food processing waste is free oil that will float to the surface. Conventional grease traps and grease-recovery systems collect free oil by allowing it to cool and float to the surface where it can be skimmed off.

3. **Chemically emulsified oil:** Modern surfactants such as detergents, high-alkaline soaps, and droplet-free rinse chemicals suspend the oil into microparticles that do not coalesce and float to the surface. These droplets, often smaller than one micron, stay suspended; no amount of time can alter that suspension

4. **Mechanically emulsified oil:** Blenders, mixers, and agitators of washing machines, as well as very hot water can suspend oil into sometimes microscopic droplets. These droplets will, given sufficient time and cooler water, coalesce and float to the surface. The problem is there is insufficient time during high-volume discharge cycles and transport to allow this coalescing to take place. This calls for surge tanks.

FOG Cutting

Removing FOGs is advantageous because (1) removal reduces the treatment time and energy to treat this dense BOD, and (2) the FOGs can be used to make biodiesel or biogas (added to a methane digester).

Most plumbing codes require commercial facilities that process or prepare food to use a grease interceptor (also known as a grease trap). This functions like a baffled septic tank, slowing the flow long enough for the solids to either sink to the bottom or float to the top. They do not work well with emulsified grease and oil, which will flow on past the baffles. Also they must be cleaned regularly by hand. Large interceptors require the services of a vacuum pump truck. Further, the unpleasant task of scooping out the grease by hand means interceptors are often neglected and subsequently fail.

A recent innovation is automatic equipment that extracts oils and greases. These systems clean themselves on a daily basis. Products such as the

Big Dipper use a skimming wheel controlled by a timer to skim the grease and oils out of the baffled chamber. The grease and oils are scrubbed off the wheel with a wiper blade and channeled out of the unit and into a collection container.

After removing as much FOG as possible, the BOD of the remaining effluent should be tested and a treatment system for that strength chosen, such as a trickling filter, aerobic or anaerobic activated sludge system, packaged treatment plant, and of course a constructed ecosystem. Keep in mind that effluent might require a nitrogen boost to achieve the 25:1 carbon-to-nitrogen ratio that allows optimal biological processing.

Graywater Use

Pretreated graywater is usually permitted for subsurface irrigation in most states. For any other purpose, it is common to use treatment standards developed by California as a model. California has been a leader in the testing and development of parameters for wastewater treatment for reuse. These standards are detailed in California Recycled Water Criteria, Title 22. According to Title 22, "Wastewater treated for reuse is called Disinfected Tertiary Recycled Water and is defined as wastewater, which has been oxidized and has been coagulated and passed through

Table 1

Chemical constituents observed in graywater in Australia and internationally								
Parameter	Abbreviation or symbol	Units	Mean	n	Min	n	Maxi	n
Suspended solids	SS	mg/L	97.4	11	2	10	1500	11
BOD5	BOD5	mg/L	530.7	7	6	7	620	7
Total organic carbon	TOC	mg/L	276.8	8	30	2	92	2
Total Kjeldahl nitrogen	TKN	mg/L		0	0.6	4	50	4
Total nitrogen	Ntot	mg/L	14.9	13	0.6	3	16	4
Ammonia	NH4-N	mg/L	2.4	23	0.06	6	25.4	14
Nitrite	NO2	mg/L		0	0	2	4.9	4
Total phosphorus	Ptot	mg/L	14.7	6	0.04	8	42	9
Phosphate	P-PO4	mg/L	34.4	13		0		0
Sulfate	SO42-	mg/L		0	4	3	168	5
pH		mg/L	7.9	3	5	13	10	13
Electrical conductivity	EC	dS/m	0.4	1	0.08	5	1.3	5
Total dissolved salts	TDS	mg/L		0	52	3	5960	3
Sodium	Na	mg/L	73.9	6	7.4	8	1090	9
Chloride	Cl	mg/L		0	3.1	3	136	3
Fluoride	F	mg/L		0	0.49	2	1.6	2
Calcium	Ca	mg/L	22.5	6	2.3	7	824	8
Magnesium	Mg	mg/L	5.1	6	0.7	7	19	8
Sodium adsorption ratio	SAR		3.6	6	0.79	7	32.2	8
Aluminium	Al	mg/L	1.5	5	0.02	2	44	6
Arsenic	As	mg/L	0.0	1	0.0002	2	0.013	3
Boron	B	mg/L	0.63	3		0		0
Cadmium	Cd	mg/L	0.0004 5	4		0	0.05	3
Copper	Cu	mg/L	0.1357	10	0.018	3	0.49	7
Cobalt	Co	mg/L	0.0009	2		0	0.0015	1
Chromium (total)	Cr	mg/L	0.0037	1		0	0.0055	1
Iron	Fe	mg/L	0.4	1	0.79	1	28	4
Mercury	Ha	mg/L		0		0	2E–05	1
Manganese	Mn	mg/L	0.023	2		0	0.0143	1
Molybenum	Mo	mg/L	0.0011	1		0		0
Nickel	Ni	mg/L	0.0110	1		0	0.028	1
Selenium	Se	mg/L	0.0002	1		0		0
Strontium	Sr	mg/L	0.0603	1		0		0
Zinc	Zn	mg/L	0.3	10	0.09	5	13	7
Potassium	K	mg/L	26	5	1.1	2	17	2
Sulfur	S	mg/L		0	1.2	2	40	2
Lead	Pb	mg/L	0.0	4		0	0.15	2

Source: A. Boal et al 1995; Department of Health WA (Australia) 2002; Eriksson et al 2002; Gardner and Millar 2003; Jeppersen and Solley 1994; Palmquist and Jönsson 2003.
n = number of sample available from the studies reviewed for a specific parameter.

natural undisturbed soils or a bed of filter media pursuant to the following:

1. At a rate that does not exceed 5 GPM/ft in mono, dual or mixed media gravity or pressure filtration systems, or does not exceed 2 GPM/ft in traveling bridge automatic backwash filters; and

2. The turbidity does not exceed any of the following; a daily average of 2 NTU, 5 NTU more than 5% of the time within a 24-hour period, and 10 NTU at any time.

Or B. It has been passed through a micro-, nano-, or reverse-osmosis membrane following which the turbidity does not exceed any of the following: 0.2 NTU more than 5% of the time within a 24-hour period and 0.5 NTU at any time, and

Or C. It has been disinfected by either:

1. A chlorine disinfection process that provides a CT of 450 mgmin/l with a modal contact time of not less than 90 minutes based on peak dry weather flow, or

2. A disinfection process that, when combined with filtration, has been demonstrated to achieve 5-log inactivation of virus."

Many forms of treatment and filtration have been approved by California. For graywater use to meet the Title 22 standard, the membrane micro-filtration and biological treatment systems seem to be the most applicable.

Packaged membrane filtration systems can achieve the oxidation and turbidity reduction in addition to the tertiary treatment requirements indicated in Title 22.

All treatment will require final disinfection by chlorine, ultraviolet light, or ozone before storage or reuse.

Table 2
Wastewater-Reuse Treatment Parameters

Parameter	Significance for Water Reuse	Range in Secondary Effluents	Treatment Goal in Reclaimed Water
Suspended solids	Measures of particles. Can be related to microbial contamination. Can interfere with disinfection. Clogging of irrigation systems. Deposition.	5 mg/L - 50 mg/L	<5 mg SS/L - 30 mg SS/L
Turbidity		1 NTU - 30 NTU	<0.1 NTU - 30 NTU
BOD$_5$	Organic substrate for microbial growth. Can favor bacterial regrowth in distribution systems as well as microbial fouling.	10 mg/L - 30 mg/L	<10 mg BOD/L - 45 mg BOD/L
COD		50 mg/L -150 mg/L	<20 mg COD/L - 90 mg COD/L
TOC		5 mg/L - 20 mg/L	<1 mg C/L - 10 mg C/L
Total coliforms	Measure of risk of infection due to potential infection. Presence of pathogens. Can favor fouling of cooling systems.	<10 cfu/100mL - 10$_7$ cfu/100mL	<1 cfu/100mL - 200 cfu/100mL
Fecal coliforms		<1-10$_6$ cfu/100mL	<1 cfu/100mL - 10$_3$ cfu/100mL
Helminth eggs		<1/L -10/L	<0.1/L - 5/L
Viruses		<1/L - 100/L	<1/50L
Heavy metals	Specific elements (Cd, Ni, Hg, Zn, etc.) are toxic to plants, and maximum concentration limits exist for irrigation.		<0.001 mg Hg/L <0.01 mg Cd/L <0.1 mg Ni/L - 0.02 mg Ni/L
Inorganics	High salinity and boron (>1 mg/L) are harmful for irrigation.		>450 mg TDS/L
Chlorine residual	To prevent bacterial regrowth. Excessive amount of free chlorine (>0.05) can damage some sensitive crops.		0.5 mg Cl/L - >1 mg Cl/L
Nitrogen	Fertilizer for irrigation. Can contribute to algal blooms and eutrophication, corrosion (N-NH4), and scale formation.	10 mg N/L - 30 mg N/L	<1 mg N - 30mgN/L
Phosphorus		0.1 mg P/L - 30 mg P/L	<1 mg P/L - 20 mg P/L

Source: Adapted from Lazarova, 2001; Metcalf and Eddy, 1991; Pettygrove and Asano, 1985

Other books by Carol Steinfeld and David Del Porto

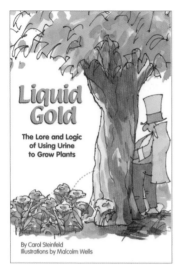

Liquid Gold
The Lore and Logic of Using Urine
to Grow Plants

by Carol Steinfeld • Illustrations by Malcolm Wells
5.25 x 8.25 • 100 pages • Many illustrations and photographs
ISBN: 978-0-9666783-1-4

Every day, we urinate nutrients that can fertilize plants that could be used for beautiful landscapes, food, fuel, and fiber. Instead, these nutrients are flushed away, either to be treated at high cost or discharged to waters where they overfertilize and choke off aquatic life.

Liquid Gold: The Lore and Logic of Using Urine to Grow Plants tells you how urine—which contains most of the nutrients in domestic wastewater and usually carries no disease risk—can be utilized as a resource. Starting with a short history of urine use—from ritual to medicinal to even culinary—and a look at some unexpected urinals, Liquid Gold shows how urine is used worldwide to grow food and landscapes, while protecting the environment, saving its users the cost of fertilizer, and reconnecting people to the land and the nutrient cycles that sustain them. That's real flower power!

Liquid Gold features several ways to use urine hygienically and productively for plant growth, with studies that show the science behind this practice. Several advocates of urine diversion and their gardens are profiled, demonstrating that using urine for fertilizer is a feasible, safe, and cost-saving way to prevent pollution and save on fertilizer costs.

Whimsical drawings by Malcolm Wells (world-renowned architect, artist, and author of several books, including *The Earth-Sheltered Home, Classic Architectural Birdhouses, Recovering America, InfraStructures,* and *How to Build an Underground House*) throughout the book make this a must for every bathroom library, a great gift for gardeners (and anyone who urinates), and an enlightening problem-solver for environmental planners dealing with the nutrient pollution of water.

Available from New Society Publishers, your favorite local bookstore, and from Ecowaters Projects:

www.ecowaters.org

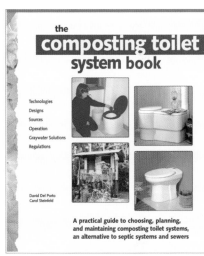

The Composting Toilet System Book

by Carol Steinfeld and David Del Porto
8.25 x 11 • 240 pages • 300 photos and diagrams
ISBN: 978-0-9666783-3-8

From cottage toilets to whole-house composters with microflush toilets and graywater gardens, *The Composting Toilet System Book* covers a wide range of ecological toilet options.

Composting toilet systems and other ecological wastewater management methods are emerging as viable and cost-saving alternatives to wastewater disposal systems. The book details why—and how to choose, install and maintain them.

The Composting Toilet System Book contains the information you need to choose and maintain composting toilet systems and other alternatives to sewer and septic systems.

- Descriptions of more than 40 systems—both manufactured and build-it-yourself—and their sources
- Compatible toilet stools and micro-flush toilet installation tips
- Tips on choosing, planning, installing and maintaining your composting toilet system
- The experiences of owner-operators worldwide
- What you should know about graywater systems
- Regulations and advice about getting your system approved

Long used by off-the-grid homeowners, parks, and cottage owners, composting toilet systems are now making their way into conventional year-round homes. The technology has improved and is available in styles compatible with upscale bathrooms. In addition to providing technical information on various systems, the book profiles composting toilet system applications worldwide, provides United States permitting information, and features key maintenance and operation information that the manufacturers do not provide. The book also contains information about using these systems with graywater systems and flush toilets. Find out how you can have a smaller leachfield, reduce pollution, and help arm yourself and your community against the skyrocketing water and sewage costs of the future.

The book is co-authored by David Del Porto, who has sold and serviced thousands of several models and brands of composting toilet systems since 1972. He has also helped write regulations and performance standards for these systems and has designed composting toilet and graywater systems for Greenpeace and for developing countries.

Available from New Society Publishers, your favorite local bookstore, and from Ecowaters Projects:

www.ecowaters.org

For updates about this book and other books by
Ecowaters, visit our Web site: www.ecowaters.org